"The premise behind *Uncommon Sense* is the biggest question in human history: Ingenious as our species may be, is it also wise enough to do what it will take to keep our civilization viable, before it's too late? Peter Seidel lays out all that ails the earth in this make-or-break century and leaves it to us to decide whether our saga continues, or ends all too soon."

—**Alan Weisman,** author of *Countdown: Our Last, Best Hope for a Future on Earth?* and *The World Without Us*

"Many years of thought, practical work, and reflection are distilled in Peter Seidel's careful analysis and urgent call to action. The book is wide-ranging and accessible to the public, yet without any 'dumbing down.' Highly recommended."

—**Herman Daly,** one of the founders of the field of ecological economics, and author of *Beyond Growth: The Economics of Sustainable Development*

"*Uncommon Sense* lays out how the human brain has both brought us to dizzying heights of technology and accomplishment and will cause our crashing demise through narcissism, violence, and ecological destruction. Its greatest contribution, however, is the vision it offers for our salvation through additional yet untapped powers of the human brain, from ecofeminism to ecotopian sci-fi literature to the Genuine Progress Indicator."

—**Kirsten Stade,** Advocacy Director, Public Employees for Environmental Responsibility (PEER)

"The author has packed this book with wisdom and insight. It highlights substantial flaws in current institutions, misguided cultural beliefs, and dangerous psychological biases, all of which hold us back from reversing the current trends toward self-destruction."

—**Mathis Wackernagel,** co-creator of the Ecological Footprint and President of the Global Footprint Network

"Peter Seidel presents a masterful tour de force in connecting the dots on how human nature is destroying Earth's nature. His topics span human instincts such as time perception and human-constructed systems in business, economics, education, politics, and religion. He makes the case that business as usual must change. Seidel states: 'We must do things differently; very differently.' The world needs to take action to make a course correction to avoid a collective planetary Titanic, and to do so, big-picture, long-term planning will be needed."

—**Janine Finnell,** Executive Director of Leaders in Energy

"We humans, making so many unsustainable choices every day, are in need of serious therapy. *Uncommon Sense* provides that therapy, boldly highlighting our failings and our potential, so that we may correct the former and reach the latter."

—**Dave Gardner,** co-host of the *GrowthBusters* podcast

"Peter Seidel takes us on an unflinching tour of humanity's 21st-century predicament: We've built a global economy that is undermining the life-support systems of the planet. Through decades of observation and independent thinking, Peter Seidel is uniquely positioned to critique our suicidal devotion to further consumption and economic growth, and to consider whether and how we can do better."

—**Rob Dietz,** coauthor of *Enough Is Enough: Building a Sustainable Economy in a World of Finite Resources*

"There is nothing to fear, not even fear. What we need to fear is complacency and ignorance. Anyone reading this book will no longer suffer from ignorance. This is a potent wake-up call because it rests on facts and data. Facts and data that tell us not what *will* be, but what *would* be *if...*"

—**Ervin Laszlo,** Founder and President of The Club of Budapest

"Seidel is a true child of the Enlightenment. A man who believes that men can think and act rationally."

—Jeffery van Davis, award-winning filmmaker, *Only God Can Save Us*

"This book combines admirable honesty about the human predicament with suggestions for regaining hope by focusing on what is realistically possible in the available time."

—Robert Engelman, former President of Worldwatch Institute

Uncommon Sense

Shortcomings of the Human Mind for Handling Big-Picture, Long-Term Challenges

By Peter Seidel

Steady State Press

© 2020 Peter Seidel

All rights reserved. No part of this publication may be reproduced, stored in a retrieval system, or transmitted in any form or by any means, electronic, mechanical, photocopying, recording, or otherwise without the prior permission of the publisher or in accordance with the provisions of the Copyright, Designs, and Patents Act 1988 or under the terms of any license permitting limited copying issues by the Copyright.

Published by:
Steady State Press
4601 N. Fairfax Dr., Suite 1200
Arlington, VA 22203
USA

Cover Design: Elisabeth Heissler

ISBN-13: 978-1-7329933-1-0

Library of Congress Control Number: 2020902567

"We have created a *Star Wars* civilization with Stone Age emotions, medieval institutions, and godlike technology."
— Edward O. Wilson

Dedicated to those who will live in the world that we leave them.

Contents

Foreword xv

Preface xix

Chapter One: From My Balcony 1
Disconnection 3
We See the Pieces and Miss the Connections 5
No One at the Helm 8

Chapter Two: The Many Problems We Face Today 11
Spotlight 2.1: Ocean Acidification 13
Our Economic Predicament 15
Our Reliance on Energy, Technology, and Natural Resources 15
Spotlight 2.2: Global Footprint and Biocapacity 16
Inequality 21
Corruption within Politics and Corporations 23
Prioritizing Peace? 24
Beyond the Sum of Problems 25

Chapter Three: What Comes with Being Human 27
Our Primitive Brain 28
Failings in Our Perception System 28
We Only Detect Short-Term Change 29
Where We Focus Our Attention 30
Our Sense of Time 31
How We Do Think 33
Spotlight 3.1: Global Population Growth 34

Clear Thinking Does Not Come Easy 36
Imagination 39
Compelling Primary Drives 40
Competitiveness 40
Spotlight 3.2: The Wealth Footprint 41
Violence 43
Avarice 49
Selfishness 50
Belief 54

Chapter Four: The Psychology of Our Modern Society 59

Social Psychology 59
Groupthink 61
Societies Ignore, Too 64
Spotlight 4.1: Today's Extinction Crisis 67
Overload 68
Ethics and Values 70
Spotlight 4.2: Beyond the Numbers 71
Religion and Other Beliefs 73
Governmental and National Ethics 75
Unintended Side Effects of Good Intentions 77
Ethics in Business 78

Chapter Five: Changing our Minds 83

Not All Responses Succeed 84
Becoming More Than What We've Been 86
Knowing How the Human Brain Works 87
Understanding Our Dependence on Nature 88
Getting Curious and Out of Denial 90
Knowing the Right Things 91

Bigger Role for Women 92
Big-Picture, Long-Term Studies 95
A Serious Role for Studying the Future 96
"A-Fiction" Literature 98
Educating Journalists 100
Moving Toward a Steady State Economy 100
Reforming Economic Policies 102
Getting Political 103
Supporting the Right Organizations 105
Keeping Our Hopes Up 106

Endnotes 109
Index 119

Figures

Figure 1. Changing landscape 2
Figure 2. Boy diamond miner in Zimbabwe 3
Figure 3. Cleared forest in Sumatra. 12
Figure 4. Global Ecological Footprint and Biocapacity. 17
Figure 5. Canadian tar sands mine. 18
Figure 6. The World Trade Center 19
Figure 7. Less fortunate Americans 20
Figure 8. *Rising Sun*, a 450-foot yacht 22
Figure 9. Historical income disparities 23
Figure 10. Global Population Landmarks 35
Figure 11. Global Population Growth 35
Figure 12. Global Ecological Footprint and Biocapacity 41
Figure 13. The World's 15 Largest Ecological Debtors 42
Figure 14. Mass Grave No. 3 at Bergen-Belsen 43
Figure 15. "The Hanging" by Jacques Callot, 1592–1635 46
Figure 16. The Arc de Triomphe in Paris 47
Figure 17. Sawing of three homosexuals from a 15th-century print. 48
Figure 18. A homeless woman sits on a street in Chicago 51
Figure 19. Fairfield Pond in the Hamptons 52
Figure 20. The Jonestown massacre 61
Figure 21. Germans giving a Nazi salute 62
Figure 22. Monthly mean atmospheric carbon dioxide 65
Figure 23. Natural and human influences on global temperature. 66
Figure 24. Malnourished children 70
Figure 25. World Wealth Report 72
Figure 26. Enjoying some of the "better" things of life 74
Figure 27. Executives from Big Tobacco 80
Figure 28. Melting glaciers 84
Figure 29. Rachel Carson 93

Foreword

I first encountered Peter Seidel at a Society of Environmental Journalists conference in Wisconsin. Or perhaps it was a conference of the U.S. Society for Ecological Economics in New York. Neither of us recall for sure, but we both noticed one thing: Our paths crossed regularly during that first decade of the 21st century. Not only did we find ourselves at the same conferences, but in the same sessions and in the same conversations—and invariably on the same side in the event of controversy or debate. Most notably, we both recognized limits to growth and the fundamental conflict between economic growth and environmental protection.

Now, I have the privilege of penning the foreword for the latest in a string of salient books in which Seidel offers a lifetime of wisdom on the "big-picture, long-term challenges" facing humanity.

Seidel is an elder statesman of limits to growth, and he had been researching, writing, and conferencing on the relevant topics for decades before I came along with my specialty on the conflict between economic growth and biodiversity conservation.

Biodiversity was big in the 1990s and early 2000s; bigger than climate change in academia and in the environmental movement. By then, though, Seidel had seen it all: DDT, a burning Cuyahoga River, Love Canal, the destruction of the ozone layer, coral bleaching, endangered species, resource shortages, and wars too numerous to speak of. Biodiversity loss and climate change were just two more insults—albeit huge ones—heaped upon a planet subjected to rabid GDP growth.

Seidel took an interest in my muffled efforts—with me in the silenced depths of the U.S. Fish and Wildlife Service at the time—to raise awareness of the trade-off between economic growth and environmental protection. He was one of the first 50 signatories of the CASSE position statement calling for a steady state economy, along with the likes of Herman Daly, William Rees, and Richard Heinberg. He was a no-nonsense, sound-science, non-fantasy futuristic thinker, and I took an interest in his work as well, reading several of his books and engaging in lengthy discussions with him on the future of America, the planet, and *Homo sapiens*.

I could see *Uncommon Sense* coming. I'd read *There is Still Time*, the predecessor book, and I knew Seidel had a rare, holistic sense of limits to growth. I was thrilled to hear of his interest in revising *There is Still Time*—which suffered from production problems and practically zero marketing—into a new book with an apropos title, updated data, and a solid plan for distribution.

With *Uncommon Sense*, I believe Seidel is at the peak of his game. It may seem a peculiar thing to say about an author in his 10th decade, but it's true in my opinion, and here's why: While Seidel's penchant for prose was fully developed by the time he wrote, for example, *Invisible Walls* (Prometheus, 1998), his inquisitive mind only found more issues to integrate in the decades since. *Uncommon Sense* packs an impressive sweep of issues into such a compact book. No book that I'm aware of melds environmental, evolutionary, psychological, social, political, and religious subject matter into one cogent, flowing analysis from a limits-to-growth lens. Certainly not in a little over a hundred pages!

The topics aren't just packed in, though, like sardines squished into some unceremonious can. Seidel has something important to say about each of these topics. While some readers will have encountered similar lines of thought on some of the topics, few readers will fail to find something original, unique, or at least new to them in the pages of this prescient book.

It's not that Seidel has all the answers, nor has he written the perfect book. (Who has?) As a student who studied the molecular basis of evolution as a supplementary topic during my Ph.D. research, I found the segments on the evolution of the human brain to be somewhat sketchy and lacking corroboration from human DNA analysis. Yet I also found myself thinking, "Maybe he doesn't have the nucleotides mapped out, but how could he possibly be wrong?" The human brain would indeed have evolved the way he described; if not, surely we'd be behaving differently.

Seidel took on a daunting challenge in writing *Uncommon Sense*. The task he bore was not simply to journalize and lament on limits to growth, but to analyze, to penetrate, to dissect what it is about *Homo sapiens* that leads us to the limits as a moth to a flame. Why don't we stop? Why *should* we? *Can we?*

The last question, of course, is the most challenging of all for any writer of such a sweeping book. In my opinion, Seidel provides a most refreshing approach. He doesn't sugarcoat the answer. You won't find any wishful notions of "green growth," "mind over matter," or "have your cake and eat it too" in *Uncommon Sense*. In his concluding chapter, Seidel comes clean on the prospects for the human race to handle the big-picture, long-term threats. The prospects, it turns out, are far from sure, easy, or even likely. It's going to take some work, folks.

But then, humans have evolved to strive, to fight, and to work. We just need to apply a little more *Uncommon Sense*.

—Brian Czech, Center for the Advancement of the Steady State Economy

Preface

Aging is not all bad. I've had the opportunity to process nine decades worth of thoughts, and one thing I do not suffer from is lack of experience. In fact, I had a life-changing experience before most of today's population was born. It was 1958, and I read *The Challenge of Man's Future* by the geochemist Harrison Brown. This book changed the course of not only my personal life, but also my professional life as an architect and urban planner. From then on I've been thinking about the big-picture, long-term prospects for *Homo sapiens*.

Disturbed by humanity's indifference to our environmental impact and, therefore, the human prospect, I wrote *Invisible Walls: Why We Ignore the Damage We Inflict on Our Planet ... and Ourselves* (Prometheus, 1998). Since then, though, humans and especially Americans have seemed to become not only indifferent, but positively resistant to doing anything significant about it. So, I resumed compiling ideas from my studies and personal observations, asking myself why we fail to live in harmony with our planet and each other. The more of these ideas I surveyed, the more clearly I saw our overall situation and the more depressed I became.

I was also somewhat confused about what to do. I knew that many environmentalists think we must always present a "positive" message to the public, to avoid "discouraging" others, so I began to question my own efforts. I wondered if I should even publish my findings, because I see little "positive" about them. If anything, the findings are disturbing and daunting, and probably discouraging. Ultimately, though, my concern is more about the earth I have loved and the people that have so much at stake with the health of the planet. I've come to the conclusion that "positive thinking" is far less important than a sober consideration of who we are, and what, if anything, we can do to change the trajectory of destruction we've heaped upon the planet. This is precisely what I've attempted to provide with *Uncommon Sense*.

Some readers may recall the title *There is Still Time*, which I published in 2015 under the imprint 360° Editions. *Uncommon Sense* is essentially *There is Still Time II*. However, only the rarest of reader—if any—would recognize it as such. *Uncommon Sense* is a completely restructured, updated, and repackaged work. Along with the newly designed cover, the subtitle *Shortcomings of the Human Mind for Handling Big-Picture, Long-Term Challenges* helps to convey the crux of the matter.

Other than one more book nearing completion (*2145*, a futuristic vision), *Uncommon Sense* is probably my last foray into the world of book publishing, and I am grateful for the encouragement and assistance of so many friends and colleagues. Some of them have left the Earth before me, but certainly I'd like to thank the likes of Lester Brown, Carol Cartaino, Rob Dietz, Robert Engleman, David Gardner, Gary Gardner, Ervin Laszlo, MaryLauren Malone, Kristen Mattis, Maggie McLaughlin, and Mathis Wackernagel.

I'd especially like to thank the outstanding staff at the Center for the Advancement of the Steady State Economy (CASSE). CASSE does more to offer a better vision for the future than any other organization I'm aware of. Brian Czech, CASSE's executive director, oversaw the revision and production of *Uncommon Sense*. Casey Reiland, CASSE's managing editor, and CASSE interns Jordan Hutchinson, Madeline Baker, and Gillian Barth provided crucial editorial assistance and updating.

Finally and most of all, I'd like to thank my wife, Angela. Although she left the world too long ago, she left it a better place.

Chapter One

From My Balcony

As I gaze out from my thirteenth floor balcony enjoying a warm summer day, it's hard to believe that I'm near the center of a metropolitan area of more than 2 million people. Most of what I see is lush and green. Trees obscure nearly all the buildings nestled on the hilltops; many more structures are tucked away in valleys hidden from me by wooded ridges. To my left, on top of a long wooded ridge, is what looks like an Italian hill town with high-rise buildings rather than fortifications. Straight ahead, a high-power electric line leads off to the west where, beyond the horizon, two columns of white smoke ascend to the sky.

A new scene appears under the fluid light of the setting sun. Darkness now hides the trees and reveals a sea of blinking lights, outlining the landscape and the two towns below. Streaming up and down the valley is a parade of yellow and red lights moving in both directions—an interstate! I watch the endless movement of the miniature cars, trucks, and motorcycles, and I have to wonder why we rely so heavily on vehicle transportation. It would save a lot of time, wear and tear, and energy if we found other methods of transportation. Not to mention, it would save our atmosphere from a huge burden of carbon dioxide. And what about the energy needed to keep all those lights on and the air conditioners running to keep us cool? I know that the power plants just over the horizon, producing the towers of smoke I saw, are being fed each and every day by the removal of mountaintops in West Virginia and eastern Kentucky to keep this whole lighted landscape, including my computer, going.

All the people out there, like myself, are linked to things we cannot see. Our genes and culture are gifts from the past, and we are making the future right now as we go about our daily business. We obtain what we need, or just desire—such as food, water, minerals, energy, the oxygen in the air, and the flowers we buy in January from other parts of the world. We burn tropical forests, converting sequestered carbon into the CO2 being released into our atmosphere; all to create grazing lands for the animals destined for our hamburgers. The cattle themselves produce huge amounts of methane, which is 84 times more potent than CO2 as a greenhouse gas.[1]

Figure 1. Changing landscape: Mountaintop removal and strip mining.
© Vivian Stockman.

And then there is what we discard. While much of it gets stowed out of sight, or dumped into waterways and carried swiftly away to the ocean, some of the most toxic substances find a home in the bodies of the world's poor who don't have access to clean water. We have regulations, laws, police, and armies trying to protect us and keep order among us; however, our efforts to protect our planet—our home and our lifeline—fall far short. Why is this so hard for us to do? This is a human shortcoming that we must explore and strive to actively rectify.

Disconnection

We are part of nature; yet few humans feel like a part of nature, much less live accordingly. Instead we see ourselves connected to the worlds of technology, money, consumerism, and entertainment. A mere hundred years ago, most people knew where their important resources came from—especially food, water, and clothing—and to a lesser degree where their waste ended up. Most of what we consumed was produced locally, and human and animal waste were returned to the soil to replenish it. Today, although waste is generated everywhere we are (and there is a lot of it!), we mostly succeed in hiding it from ourselves. Copious waste weighs heavily on the environment, poisoning the air, land, soil, and our water supplies.

Figure 2. Boy diamond miner in Zimbabwe.
© Robin Hammond/Panos.

Today we are mentally and often physically disconnected from the root sources of the food, energy, and materials we consume, as well as the places our waste ends up. When we buy milk or strawberries at a supermarket, we don't know where they come from, nor do we care.

Traditionally (and today in farmers' markets) we purchased food from the people who produced it. More recently, we could walk to a grocery store to shop for food, and often stores would deliver right to our homes. Since then, the nearby grocery has been replaced by a neighborhood supermarket and again by a Megamart or a "supercenter" designed to dazzle buyers and save distribution costs for merchants. Though the merchants slash their costs, the Megamart hikes up infrastructural costs for driving, requires more parking lots, and demands more roads for us to get there. The dazzle has blinded most of us to environmental costs as well as to personal costs of time and money. We are turning farmland that will soon be needed for feeding ever more people into pavement and rooftops. In the process, we are consuming ever more fossil fuels—and emitting ever more greenhouse gases—to keep food on our tables.

When we buy a diamond ring or gold pendant, we don't see the cruelties imposed on largely African miners, some of whom are children, and some of whom are slaves, nor do we see the corruption in their countries caused by warlords and criminal mine operators. Likewise, when we jump in our car to go for a drive, we fail to connect the exhaust that trails behind us to the melting of glaciers in the Himalayas. Nor do we consider the fact that the money we spend at the pumps is helping Saudi Wahhabis fund religious schools where a vile corruption of Islam is taught along with hate, and where future terrorists are inspired.

We spend most of our lives in artificial environments, see attractively packaged food coming from supermarkets, and are oblivious to the places and people who produced it. We vacation in far-off places we often know better than the countryside around our community and maybe even our own backyards!

We have long forgotten—if we've ever known—the sights, sounds, and smells of the natural world that keeps us alive.

Our planet, and even our species, has been here for a long time, but for us, reality is "now." We fail to ponder long-term trends, even as they play out every day. Unless the change is right in front of our eyes, we think of yesterday as an earlier version of today. We don't notice that today on Earth we have 385,000 more people than yesterday, while approximately 15,000 children under the age of five died yesterday as a result of malnutrition. We are oblivious to the fact that yesterday, 4,320 acres of arable land were degraded or abandoned to agriculture, while 200,000 acres of rainforest were obliterated.[2] Given that we know none of these things, how would we know that, today, the same losses (and then some) are occurring? While many people have heard such facts, few of us give them more than a fleeting thought or grasp their significance. They just don't sink in.

Even if everyone lived like Europeans, who consume and pollute a lot less than Americans do, we would require 2.8 planets like our own to supply our current rates of resource consumption.[3] Most people feel (if they think about it at all) that they can continue to get by exploiting our planet and overlooking the plight of the unfortunate for a few more decades. If we don't personally and currently see or feel the consequences of our unconscious actions, we tend to ignore them, even if the warnings are profoundly relevant to our quality of life and the survival of generations to come.

We See the Pieces and Miss the Connections

As a boy I would stand on street corners in my hometown of Milwaukee and imagine what the scene before me would have been like 50 years before, and would be like 50 years in the future. I was disturbed by all the automobiles I saw around me burning up what I knew was a limited resource, and I could envision the ambulances and fire engines of the future without any gas left in the world to fuel them—stuck. My interest in the connection between how our present-day actions influence the structure and function of our society in the future eventually drew me to a career in architecture and city planning. I enjoyed and saw the importance of seeing buildings and cities as unified systems, and was fascinated by evaluating their influence on people as well as how they would fit into and affect their surroundings. Essentially, my time as an architect and city planner led me to a critical conclusion: Almost everything in our world is in some way connected to most everything else.

For reasons we will explore later on, we humans do not view or see the world as an integrated whole. Instead we observe it as if we are looking through a tube focusing on one tiny piece at a time. Many of us are very skilled and knowledgeable in one or a few small areas. Our competence in that one area often provides us with the illusion that we understand a lot more than we do. By focusing attention on very small pieces of reality, exceptional individuals have developed an incredible knowledge about genes, string theory, and dark matter, and have developed and advanced remarkable capabilities in fields like nanotechnology and space exploration. Taking a step back and reflecting upon how we are utilizing this knowledge in dealing with one another and our planet, we can see that it is sometimes wonderful and other times awful. Our technology, though it might have been created with the best of intentions, gives us an overwhelming impact on our surroundings, and the combination of ignorance, arrogance, and technology is leading us toward serious trouble.

Although we try to view our complex world compartmentally, the planet is simply not structured that way. Every little action, object, or resource, is connected. The basic idea of our interconnectedness stems from our planet's biosphere, which in and of itself is an integrated whole whose parts work together to maintain the milieu we live in.

The intricate working parts of our biosphere are not only connected with each other in the present, but also to parts in the past and the future as well. To truly understand the state of our world today and the impact of our human influence, we have to understand our history and evolutionary past. Sadly, as links in a chain and beneficiaries of our past and present, we show little concern for those who will follow.

Understanding the planet's innate harmony may be a more difficult concept to grasp, especially with our failure to see more obvious connections. Continuous population increase and economic growth on a finite planet is impossible. Even many environmentalists ignore this truth. It's as if questioning economic growth is taboo. Whether from fear or ignorance, the silence on this matter is creating serious consequences around the globe.

The bottom line is that we have trouble connecting, recalling, and utilizing information, significant as it may be, that is not clearly related to our own personal situations. Most economists, politicians, and businesspeople would know (hopefully!) that neither population nor the economy can grow indefinitely. Yet when there is a lack of economic growth or a discussion about controlling birth rates, these figureheads raise alarm. They are only aware of the benefits of perpetual growth as taught in conventional economics, which has not yet progressed to deal with limits to growth and the need for a steady state economy.

Additionally, the majority of these leaders rely on economic growth for personal profit and political advancement. They spend no time learning how economic growth impacts our environment—because they don't have to. Yet voters elect such environmentally oblivious politicians to positions of high power due to little more than persuasive rhetoric. Once elected, they reinforce the rhetoric that we can have our cake and eat it too; that we can grow the economy and protect the environment all at once.

It's no surprise then that we struggle with accepting the root causes of our environmental problems. Even when presented with indisputable facts, we still shy away from recognizing our faults when it comes to the deterioration of the planet. For instance, in 1970 Paul Ehrlich and John Holdren presented a simple formula called "IPAT," or:

$$I = P \times A \times T$$

> *The IPAT formula summarizes our environmental impacts succinctly. I = impact, P = population, A = affluence (consumption per capita), and T = technology.*[4]

If everything stays the same but the world population doubles, humanity's impact on the planet doubles. Similarly, if everything stays the same but personal consumption doubles, humanity's impact on the planet doubles. On the other hand, if everything is done twice as efficiently, humanity's impact on the planet is cut in half. Although this equation is simple and clear enough, we ignore it. It's easy to suggest improving technology, but seriously discussing population reduction is taboo, and who dares to suggest that we consume less? Furthermore, when we generate more technology, we instantly use it for more consumption!

Limiting our thinking to pieces, rather than the whole picture, pays off individually. Focusing one's knowledge, expertise, and efforts in a narrow area avoids distractions, simplifies work, brings one success in one's field, and can make one famous or a multimillionaire. Conversely, considering the big picture and all of its problems is not valued and creates no immediate benefit, leaving this generalist perspective out of important decisions that affect us all.

No One at the Helm

Ant colonies, beehives, groups of human hunter-gatherers, and our cities and nations are organized at various levels. With all the remarkable technology we have developed, the information that is available, and the organization we have put in place, it would be reasonable to think that our fast-paced consumer lifestyle is sensible. As a child I thought that "grown-ups" were wise, understood everything, and knew what was best for all of us. Then I grew up and learned that there is no wise person, group, or organization that is managing our essential resources and needs in a world where we have demolished the barriers that once kept us in balance with our environment.

This pro-growth world we've created is driven by uncoordinated, primitive human drives that are, at times, tempered by reason. The frenzy of economic activity is a combination of many unconnected, uncoordinated efforts mostly working to meet short-term, individual wants and needs. Most people focus their attention and concerns on the well-being of their family, close associates, and themselves, giving little thought to the overall good or the future.

Instead of attempting to make changes, we rely on information handed to us from a wide variety of authority figures, each with their own biased personal agendas. Brash "free marketers" claim that this pursuit of self-interest is Adam Smith's "invisible hand" working as self-organization for the overall good. Conventional economists, bankers, business leaders, and politicians laud our egoism for putting and keeping us on track for economic growth. We plunge ahead ignoring warnings that all is not OK.

We are essentially a mindless mass with tremendous power in our hands, but without unified, selfless leadership. We are like a bull in a china shop, seemingly unaware of the havoc we are creating. We all know a lot of what I will be describing in the following chapters, but we tend to view it in pieces, so we don't see the scope of the problem, the big picture. To get that, we must put the pieces together and look at the world and our society as a connected, whole system: our primitive tendencies, human psychology, the harm caused by self-interest, the planetary impacts of our ignorance, and, hopefully, the solutions we can offer to amend them.

Chapter Two

The Many Problems We Face Today

Until humans took up agriculture around 10,000 years ago, they lived within the confines of a hunter-gatherer niche. Agriculture and other innovations, and later modern medicine, enabled the human population to grow enormously, putting it at odds with other forms of life. Today, agriculture is our most basic source of sustenance, but poor farming practices have stripped the land of productive topsoil and depleted aquifers around the world. We typically believe that our human impact on the environment is recent, but harmful methods of farming appeared early on in human history, specifically in such places as ancient Greece, North Africa, China's Yellow River basin, and pre-Columbian Central America. Salinization of soils ruined irrigation agriculture in Mesopotamia and the Indus Valley. Rampant population growth, deforestation, and topsoil erosion caused the Mayan and Easter Island civilizations to collapse.

Stripping away land is not only detrimental to food production; it is also killing off species. We are now changing the environment so rapidly that many species cannot adapt fast enough to survive. We are losing species between 10 to 100 times faster than the average rate of extinction over the last 10 million years, and that rate is accelerating.[5] Thousands of plant and animal species are disappearing, and soon there will not be enough habitats left to support large carnivores in the wild.

Though we encourage agricultural innovation and productivity, we think little about how our ongoing farming practices impact the rest of the ecological system. And although many of our ancestors have endured the heavy costs of these detrimental practices, we take no heed of their experiences, and we continue to carry on without recognizing the severity of the damage we inflict. During the last several centuries, we have developed a staggering collection of new technologies and devices that have accelerated the expansion of our niche and our impact on the planet even further. It's become a tradition of unchecked egocentrism.

Figure 3. Cleared forest in Sumatra. © Melvinas Priananda, Greenpeace.

I find it astounding that there are four times as many people on this planet than when I was born in 1926! Growing numbers of people demanding ever more things and creating ever more waste and pollution have so rapidly overburdened our planet. Now, with our burgeoning population, the harm we are doing to our planet is increasing exponentially. Our limitless thirst for fossil fuels is depleting irreplaceable resources, and one of the things we get in return is climate change. This is hardly a good deal when we translate "climate change" into the more tangible effects of extreme weather, rising sea levels, and ocean acidification that destroys coral reefs and fishery food webs. Water contamination and shortages, deforestation, loss of cropland, soil erosion, and ecosystem deterioration threaten food production for a human population that only continues to grow. All of this forces mass migration of people from areas that can no longer support and sustain them.

SPOTLIGHT 2.1: Ocean Acidification

The world's oceans are 30 percent more acidic than before the Industrial Revolution, the product of steadily rising levels of pollution. Carbon emissions are a key concern: The oceans are a major depository of carbon, and about a quarter of humanity's annual atmospheric emissions of carbon end up there. CO_2 reacts with seawater to lower the pH (raise the acidity) of the water. Today's acidification rate is estimated to be 10 to 100 times faster than at any time in the past 50 million years. Acidification causes the shells and skeletons of "marine calcifiers"—corals, oysters, clams, mussels, and snails, in addition to phytoplankton and zooplankton that form the base of the marine food web—to dissolve more readily as seawater becomes more corrosive from acidification. By the middle of the century, oceanic accumulation of carbon dioxide is likely to be twice as great as prior to the industrial era, creating increased acidification pressures. Indeed, at continued high rates of carbon emissions, acidity could increase by 170 percent by 2100.

Oceanic history provides clear warning signs of the harm from acidification. An increase in atmospheric carbon and oceanic acidification 55 million years ago—at rates far slower than today's—produced a mass extinction of some marine species, especially deep-sea shelled invertebrates. Meanwhile, the Intergovernmental Panel on Climate Change observes that acidification of oceans over the rest of the century could produce ocean changes similar to those observed during the event 55 million years ago.

> For all the trouble that ocean acidification portends, it is also credited with slowing the rate at which the planet is warming because oceans have taken up carbon that would otherwise have remained in the atmosphere. But this blessing is likely to diminish: As the world's oceans warm and become saturated with carbon, the rate of accumulation is projected to fall.
>
> **Literature Cited**
>
> "Ocean acidification," The National Oceanic and Atmospheric Administration, last updated on April 2020, https://www.noaa.gov/education/resource-collections/ocean-coasts/ocean-acidification.
>
> "Ocean Acidification," Woods Hole Oceanographic Institution, accessed on September 28, 2020, https://www.whoi.edu/main/topic/ocean-acidification.
>
> "20 Facts about Ocean Acidification," Woods Hole Oceanographic Institution, November 2013, https://www.whoi.edu/fileserver.do?id=165564&pt=2&p=150429.

Today, through the publication of regular updates on scientific research, we are learning that many of these problems are worse than we had previously thought. In 2010 we learned that stocks of phytoplankton had decreased by 40 percent since 1950, most likely as a result of global warming.[6] Phytoplankton is the foundation for all the oceans' food chains. Polar ice caps and glaciers worldwide are disappearing, and ocean acidification is increasing much faster than previously predicted. We have already extinguished close to a thousand species—not including invertebrates and plants—and many more will soon disappear as our population grows and we increase our burden on the earth. All of this will have grave consequences for life in the oceans and for humankind.

Our Economic Predicament

We have an economic and financial system that, in order to be maintained, depends on perpetual growth in a finite space. In the early 1970s our planet passed beyond the point of environmental sustainability. Our ecological footprint surpassed the earth's ecological capacity and put us into ecological debt.[7] We have extinguished entire species and used far more resources than our ecosystems can renew. Still at every waking hour, businesses, governments, and many of us as individuals call for more growth. To get out of recessions and return to this excessive and detrimental growth, businesses and governments believe they must lay people off from commendable occupations such as education, scientific research, environmental protection, the arts, and health care—the core civic aspects of our society that are essential in keeping us healthy and engaged with one another. We are not making an effort to solve this dilemma because we hold our economic system to be sacrosanct, no matter how ridiculous the results.

Yes, we won the Cold War, and capitalism does amazingly well at producing goods and services. But how much did we win, when capitalism ignores the limitations of our planet and the needs of the less fortunate? It is now driving us along a path toward inevitable collapse. As people are laid off, capitalists strive for higher worker productivity. This means that production, consumption, waste, and damage to nature will have to increase significantly just to keep people employed. It's futureless growth, as it depletes the resources future generations could have used for *their* economies.

Our Reliance on Energy, Technology, and Natural Resources

Society is progressively making itself more vulnerable to crisis. We are increasing our dependence on inexpensive energy and vast transportation networks, as well as complex technology requiring highly trained technicians. Our vulnerability is especially pronounced in the healthcare and food supply systems,

SPOTLIGHT 2.2: Global Footprint and Biocapacity

Human societies make large and growing demands on the goods and services our planet provides—from food, fish, and water to ecological services such as absorption of carbon dioxide. But how much demand is too much?

Global Footprint Network, an international sustainability think tank, maintains and updates the National Footprint Accounts calculations. These calculations assess the planet's biological capacity, or biocapacity. Global Footprint Network's latest published data shows global biocapacity to be 12 billion hectares. This is the natural endowment available to support human and other forms of life on the planet. Meanwhile, humanity's Ecological Footprint is the biologically productive area needed to accommodate human demands for nature's goods and services. For 2008, this number was 18.2 billion hectares.

Thus, humanity's demands on the planet's biocapacity are about 50 percent greater than our planet can renew—in other words, it takes about one year and six months to regenerate what people demand from nature in one year. The only way to sustain this ecological overspending is by digging into nature's capital accounts. We catch more fish than the oceans can regenerate and we cut forests faster than they can grow back. This is not a lasting strategy: Eventually fishing areas will be empty and forested areas will be gone. Even if complete exhaustion of resources is decades away, the impacts of overexploitation are felt much sooner, often in the form of soaring prices for resources.

Global Footprint Network describes nations that use more ecological resources than their ecosystems can renew as "ecological debtors." Whereas most societies through most of history were "ecological creditors," today 85 percent of the world population lives in countries that are ecological debtors. And the global population as a whole is running an ecological deficit.

Humanity's Ecological Footprint has fluctuated somewhat over time, while our planet's biocapacity has declined as ecosystems are degraded and lost.

> By the early 1970s, the global Ecological Footprint had surpassed the Earth's biocapacity, and the gap between the two—the ecological debt incurred by humanity—has grown larger since then. We are in ecological overshoot. (See Figure 6.)
>
> **Figure 4. Global Ecological Footprint and Biocapacity. Global Footprint Network, 2016.**
>
> **Literature Cited**
>
> Rees, W. and M. Wackernagel. 2013. The shoe fits, but the footprint is larger than Earth. *PLOS Biology* 11(11).
>
> "Data and Methodology," Global Footprint Network, accessed on September 28, 2020, https://www.footprintnetwork.org/resources/data/.
>
> "Ecological Footprint," Global Footprint Network, accessed on September 28, 2020, https://www.footprintnetwork.org/our-work/ecological-footprint/.

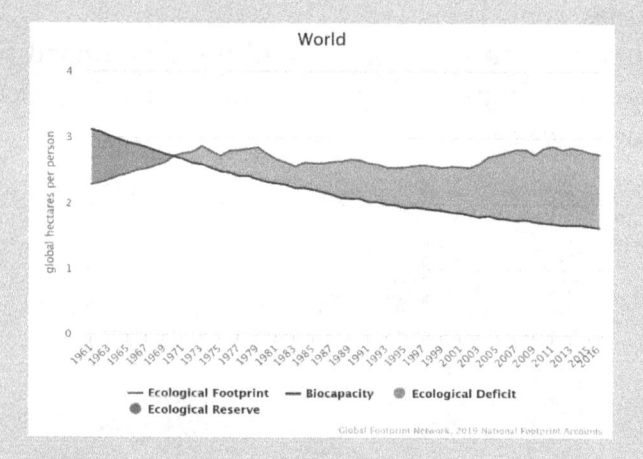

yet we give little thought to what can happen if catastrophes of environmental and international conflict overlap. It would be wise to give our vulnerabilities a serious look.

Our dependence on electricity is perhaps the most prominent. Contemporary society, particularly in urban areas, simply cannot function without electricity. People depending on systems such as subways cannot get about their daily lives without it. Those with cars would find driving a disaster without traffic signals and streetlights, and they would be shocked to find that gas stations could no longer pump fuel from their underground tanks without electrical service. Food stores would be dark, and refrigerated food would soon start to spoil. Heating, cooling, ventilation systems, and elevators in high-rise buildings would soon stop.

Without electricity, water could not be pumped to upper floors of buildings, leaving people thirsty and exposed to the backup of sewage.

Figure 5. Canadian tar sands mine. © Jiri Rezac/Polaris.

Unexpected problems arise in the absence of electricity. As an architect, I once worked on an office building in Tulsa, Oklahoma, where the air conditioning went off and the building had to be evacuated because there was no way to open the windows! We have to wonder what other surprises may lie in store, when our over-extended electricity demands cannot be met.

Unguarded electric power grids are prime targets for physical and cyber attacks by terrorists, as well as demand overload and natural threats such as solar storms. The geomagnetic disturbance of 1859, referred to as "the Carrington Event," induced currents so powerful that telegraph lines, towers, and stations caught fire in numerous areas around the world.[8] In 1989, a severe solar storm induced powerful electric currents in grid wiring that fried a main power transformer in the HydroQuebec system, causing a cascading grid failure that knocked out power to 6 million customers for nine hours.[9] Such transformers cost well over a million dollars each, and there was a three-year waiting list for new ones.[10] A massive solar storm could even trigger an environmental catastrophe, because reliable power-grid circuitry is required for cooling spent nuclear fuel rods.

We have also become more susceptible to cyber dangers within the past decade. A major computer virus, malware, worm, logic bomb, rigged chips, cyber attack, or cyber war between nations has the potential to create havoc in anything connected to the internet. Communications, power grids, global positioning systems, financial accounts, government files, military secrets, scientific data, medical records, proprietary information, personal data storage, and transactions are all vulnerable.

Figure 6. The World Trade Center ablaze with the Statue of Liberty in the foreground. © User 9/11 Photos on Flickr.com.

Whereas city-states were once protected by walls, and nations by the complex hardware of weapons systems, a cyber attack ignores walls and creeps into hardware one electron at a time. Governments and corporations are aware of these dangers. However, considering their penchant for short-term solutions, can we count on them to address the full extent of the risks and to cover the costs of mitigating them?

Furthermore, our weapons have developed in more ways than we ever could have imagined mere decades ago—ways that pose a serious threat to the environment. Clubs, spears, and bows and arrows can do great damage to individuals, but they don't harm our planet. We have stored chemicals, Agent Orange for example, that can devastate entire landscapes, and nuclear weapons that could easily usher us into a nuclear winter.

The Cold War ended in 1991, at which time the Soviet Union and the USA had huge stockpiles of nuclear weapons. Although reductions in inventory were made, these weapons were far from banished. Nineteen years later, in 2010, Barack Obama and Dmitry Medvedev signed a treaty "reducing" the number of operational strategic nuclear weapons—to 1,550.[11] And this was between two countries at peace with each other for over 20 years!

Figure 7. Less fortunate Americans. © Steve Liss.

Of course there are other countries with nuclear weapons to worry about, but looking back at Hiroshima, what kind of logic demands that we retain 1,550 of these bombs, some of which are hundreds of times more powerful than the one that destroyed Hiroshima? Having visited Hiroshima and its museum, and viewed films of the city's destruction, it is incomprehensible to me that any of these weapons can be found acceptable.

Meanwhile the development, production, and maintenance of such weapons diverts funds and resources from human needs and protecting the environment.

Finally, we are not only vulnerable to man-made creations and acts of God but also to the abuses we have heaped upon the natural world. Given the size of the global population and economy, surface and groundwater stocks are essential for human consumption, agriculture, and industry, but shortages threaten huge regions already and pollution threatens many remaining sources.

Similarly, fossil fuels are rapidly becoming depleted, with occasional bouts of "plenty" due to extreme extractionary methods such as fracking. The long-term trend is inexorably down, though, and without cheap liquid fuels, our complex transportation system gets too expensive to support the delivery of goods and services we're accustomed to. The production of ethanol is already competing with the land needed to grow food for livestock and even directly for humans.

In his book, *Storms of My Grandchildren*, the renowned climate scientist James Hansen warned, "I've come to conclude that if we burn all reserves of oil, gas, and coal, there is a substantial chance we will initiate the runaway greenhouse. If we also burn the tar sand and tar shale, I believe the Venus syndrome [a super-heated, lifeless planet] is a dead certainty."[12] To obtain natural gas and petroleum through fracking, we're adding toxins and pumping huge amounts of water, badly needed for a litany of other purposes, into the ground and rapidly mining tar sands.

Without petroleum, the feedstock for our plastics industry, we will have to resort or revert to using metals, wood, or even hides. Meanwhile, high-yield grains—essential now and only more so as the population grows—rely on artificial fertilizer, pesticides, herbicides, farm machinery, and complex delivery networks. All of these entail copious quantities of fossil fuels.

Inequality

Some people accumulate millions of dollars a year—billions

even—while many, especially in underdeveloped regions, do not have enough to eat. They lack schools, medical care, and clean water to drink. As the rich try to outdo each other by buying extravagant yachts they rarely use, showing off with diamonds and gold, approximately 15,000 children under the age of five die each day due to malnutrition.[13]

Figure 8. *Rising Sun,* a 450-foot yacht co-owned by Larry Ellison and David Geffen. The yacht is equipped with jacuzzi bathrooms, a gym, spa salons, a huge wine cellar, a private cinema with a giant plasma screen, and a basketball court on the main deck which also serves as a helicopter pad. © Giorgio Ferretto.

Many corporate executives see themselves as the benefactors of society. The Walton family, for example, might recognize the thousands who they've employed, and feel that they have contributed to society in providing jobs, but they neglect many others who have lost their jobs as Walmarts put the mom-and-pop retailers out of business. Certain groups of people feel that they deserve their wealth because of their services to society, but they are simply perpetuating wealth inequality. Millions of Americans go to bed hungry, in debt, and in financial uncertainty every night because a tiny number of entertainers, musicians, and sports stars garner a larger share of income and assets leaving others to languish. How far can this trend continue before the "winners" no longer seem so heroic to the "losers?"

To put it bluntly, greed is one of the root causes of our inequality problem. It perpetuates inequality and supersedes concern for others today as well as the children of the future. In the USA the gap between the rich and poor has been widening (Figure 9). If this trend continues we will become a very different kind of country than the one envisioned by our founding fathers. This could conceivably end in revolution. It may seem preposterous to the complacent or the distracted, but once upon a time French nobles, Russian tsars, and Chinese imperialists, too, thought it preposterous that the downtrodden masses could ever revolt. As inequality becomes extreme, revolution of some shape or form becomes not only conceivable; it is entirely precedented and practically predictable.

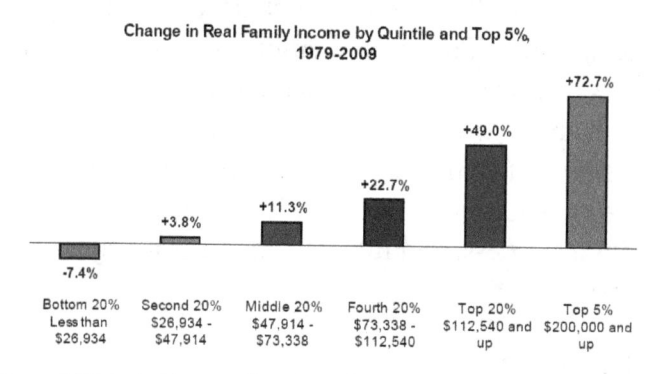

Change in Real Family Income by Quintile and Top 5%, 1979-2009

Bottom 20% Less than $26,934	Second 20% $26,934 - $47,914	Middle 20% $47,914 - $73,338	Fourth 20% $73,338 - $112,540	Top 20% $112,540 and up	Top 5% $200,000 and up
-7.4%	+3.8%	+11.3%	+22.7%	+49.0%	+72.7%

Figure 9. Historical income disparities. Source: U.S. Census Bureau.

Corruption within Politics and Corporations

Considerable damage is sustained and a huge amount of time, energy, and financial resources are consumed dealing with the consequences of lying, stealing, cheating, and corruption. The temptation to "grease the wheels" is pervasive, even among reasonably honest people. In some societies, favors are an essential way of getting things done. When I spent time in China and India teaching urban planning, "favors" were taken for granted by virtually everyone. Sometimes American businesses trying to get contracts in foreign countries simply cannot get government business without making payoffs.

In the USA, legislators are taken on golf outings and to expensive restaurants. Pharmaceutical companies entertain doctors and take them on vacations, etc. Political contributions by lobbyists, individuals, and interest groups are simply payments to get something done a certain way.

These corporations and people within them use their underhanded tactics to influence the general population as well. With the help of Madison Avenue advertising firms, they work on our emotions to sell us things. They often lie about the safety of their products and occasionally fund organizations to mislead us on the environmental and social effects of their products and industries.

Similarly, politicians (often with strong corporate ties) cynically arouse primitive feelings such as fear, bigotry, and greed. By evoking some of our basest emotions, they often succeed in getting us to vote against our own morals and interests.

Citizens, meanwhile, are not all innocent bystanders. We are often guilty of taking the path of least resistance. We accept the lies of corporations and politicians because of our apathy, intellectual laziness, and inclination to put an agenda ahead of the evidence.

Prioritizing Peace?

Most people desire a world of peace, and in *The Better Angels of Our Nature: Why Violence Has Declined*, psychologist Steven Pinker presents clear evidence that despite our violent past and what takes place today, the world is actually much less violent than it was in the past.[14] He points out that as people join together into continually growing units leading up to our nation-states today with many international agreements and global trade, cooperation becomes more important. Although violence is still far too common, most governments and businesses depend on and promote peace.

Why, then, are we still plagued with such hostility and warfare? Where is the long-awaited "peace dividend"? International conflicts divert attention and resources away from critical needs such as environmental problems, education, reducing inequality, and introducing a more stable, equitable economic system. An answer to our hostility question might be that for many countries, especially the USA, it's easier to gain support for combating ruthless leaders, such as Kim Jong-un and warlords in Somalia, than for climate research and other more nuanced issues.

As of 2018, for each dollar of federal income tax Americans pay, the government spends 24 cents on the military, half of which goes to private contractors.[15] If citizens are so worried about their national debt, then why do they support sending troops abroad and spending billions of dollars on the military when many of our economic and environmental needs could be rectified with that same amount of effort?

Beyond the Sum of Problems

The issues today are so intertwined and complex, and so much is still unknown about the rapidly multiplying problems we face, that it is impossible to get an overall picture of what is taking place in our world. While some of the problems we face appear manageable, when they interact and exacerbate each other, the consequences become considerably worse than the simple "sum" of the problems themselves. José Ortega y Gasset, the Spanish liberal philosopher and essayist, warned us in 1930, "The disproportion between the complex subtlety of the problems and the minds that should study them will become greater if a remedy be not found, and it constitutes the basic tragedy of our civilization."[16]

So, now we are faced with a plethora of daunting problems that stem from our very nature. When we look as honestly as we can at our past and present, and connect the dots among all the problems, we sketch a picture of ourselves. Yet we seldom attempt such an analysis. Instead, our human nature has us thinking in the here and now, and merely in terms of what is visible to us.

The problems we are creating, for ourselves and for generations to come, are far-reaching and often not visible until the advanced stages. Furthermore, it takes the eye of time to "see" such disastrous processes as climate change, sea-level rise, and the extinction of species. By taking a step back and observing what's going on in the world, as objectively as we can, we see that our species is bringing on its own demise. The process appears slow from the perspective of our daily routine, but it is frighteningly fast in evolutionary time. We are like passengers on a bus in which most of us don't know or care where we are headed, but we enjoy the ride and keep calling for more speed. The few who complain or ask for clarification are labeled killjoys, "nuts," or alarmists, and summarily dismissed. Whatever survival instinct we have doesn't seem to cover our kids or grandkids. We need to stop the bus and think our way out of this predicament, for their sake if not for ours.

Chapter Three

What Comes with Being Human

We seem to be a society of narcissists. Just take one look at a magazine stand—models line every glossy page with perfect hair, clear skin, and a flawless physique. Or listen to a news station, where politicians boast of how well their countries are doing, how despite the multitude of daunting challenges at the global level, their nations' economies and militaries are bigger and stronger than ever. Not that most of us care much about the nation, either, or its institutions. We're invested in our own personal problems, usually not bothering to listen to the struggles of others. We boast of our achievements, believing that the strides we've made are remarkable. For the most part, we've come to accept our egocentrism as the natural way to be. Rarely do we consider why.

To analyze our behaviors, we must look internally. Doing so means we have to eliminate the constant distractions, temporarily at least. Let's try it. Let's pause to go on an introspective journey. It's time now to move inward and pull to the surface our basic drives and emotions, to understand who we really are and how we can control them to transform our outward forces toward more positive outcomes.

Our Primitive Brain

Edward O. Wilson summarized our predicament succinctly: "We have created a *Star Wars* civilization with Stone Age emotions, medieval institutions, and godlike technology."[17] Coupling powerful tools and weapons with hunter-gatherer minds is a recipe for disaster.

Our brains' basic structure comes from an ancient evolutionary past. Though it has developed immensely over time, it still harbors drives from a hunter-gatherer mindset, and even earlier survival instincts. It is amazing that, with such limitations, the human brain gave rise to modern civilization. Unfortunately, we are not doing as good a job of managing this civilization, and it is now threatening our future. Our contemporary lives have left our brains behind; the way we use them makes us dangerous misfits in the new environment we have created. We must consciously override habitual ways of thinking that prevent us from working together to safely coexist with one another and our planet today.

Our brains have served us well until recent centuries. Acting the way we once did, with survival and reproduction at the core of all action, may now lead to our extinction. We need to understand why this is so. We will start by looking at the human perception system.

Failings in Our Perception System

How we interact with our world depends on how we perceive it, and often our view of reality is skewed. I live among a very small percent of humanity that became extremely wealthy in a tiny fragment of time. This seems normal to me. I am an honest person and although I know better, I am, like many others, subject to the false-consensus bias: The impression that others think like I do. It takes vigilance on my part to fight this and avoid being taken advantage of. I have known "operators" who distrust everyone, and they lead their lives accordingly.

Our different perspectives affect our interactions and create misunderstandings among ourselves.

In the ancient past, we did not need an awareness of processes such as the carbon cycle, which is essential for all life on the planet. The climate was self-regulating and hardly affected by human economic activity; after all we weren't burning fossil fuels back then. But today, we are loading our atmosphere with greenhouse gases by burning immense quantities of fossil fuels and burning up the earth's vegetation all in the pursuit of economic growth. It has taken us a long time to learn that we are also extinguishing countless species of plants and animals. Although we are learning about the environmental degradation we've caused and continue to commit, our responses are half-hearted because we do not yet feel the consequences.

We are now living in an environment that is rapidly teetering out of balance, but we have no natural cognitive mechanism to adequately alarm us about the dangers that lie ahead. Our mental images of reality omit much of the data we need in order to understand this situation and deal with it safely.

We Only Detect Short-Term Change

Our perception system only responds to differences such as a change in color or intensity in our visual field, or a change in volume or pitch in sound. If there is no change, we notice nothing. Similarly, if the change is gradual or slight, it passes unnoticed, as the creeping cheetah goes unnoticed by the feeding gazelle.

In ancient times, people did not need to be aware of slow change, such as the melting of glaciers and the rising of sea levels. Today it is essential that we notice the changes we are inflicting on the planet that will substantially impact our environment over the coming years, no matter how irrelevant they may seem now. Like a frog in a pot of slowly heating water, unaware of the danger until it's too late, few people notice the accumulating consequences of how we live our lives. Often, because it makes us feel good, we are the ones who "turn up the heat." We want to buy convertibles, own mansions, and purchase the latest "smart" device despite the clear ecological damage we choose to ignore, so we keep spending and expanding. As a result, our ecological footprint keeps growing while nature keeps receding. We want more automobiles, fast food, and a dizzying display of disposable items: cups, razors, straws, wrappers, utensils, bags, boxes, coffee packets, filters, towels, cans, bottles, diapers, and the truly ridiculous amounts of packaging used to display and ship disposable and nondisposable items alike.

Where We Focus Our Attention

A serious problem with many people today is that when they hear about climate change, or a prolonged drought in a distant country, they simply are not moved. Our relative indifference to the environment beyond our immediate surroundings lies deep within us. The human brain evolved to commit itself emotionally and logically to only a small piece of geography along with a limited band of kinsmen. Evolution shaped us to value what is close to us in time and space. That was essential for hunter-gatherers, who focused their interest on their sources of food, surroundings, family, neighbors, the weather . . . things directly connected to their physiological needs and welfare. Edward O. Wilson put it this way:

> For hundreds of millennia those who focused on short-term gains within a small circle of relatives and friends lived longer and left more offspring—even when their collective striving caused their chiefdoms and empires to crumble around them. The long view that might have saved their distant descendants required a vision and extended altruism instinctively difficult to marshal.[18]

Furthermore, our visual sense of perspective makes an object that is far from us appear smaller than it actually is. An automobile bearing down on me is very real and needs my attention; even a tank two miles away does not. We need to start realizing that the intensity of our perception of something is not necessarily in direct proportion to the importance of the thing itself. Even though we may not perceive it, we are so connected to events far away and in the future that it's reckless to distance ourselves from these realities.

In other words, we now live in a social environment where our feelings about an event can be totally unrelated to its importance. Yet we ignore our own relationship to distant conditions. Many of us are unmoved or even pleased when the U.S. government cuts foreign aid that was earmarked for malnourished children.

Little local stories often touch us while global crises do not. We are more moved when a cute dog is hit by a car than by the fact that a million children are facing starvation in another part of the world. Much less are we concerned over the deterioration of our planet. GDP growth estimates for the next quarter get more of our attention than issues of global environmental problems that profoundly threaten the health and wellbeing of our next generation.

Our Sense of Time

We have a poor comprehension of time, or interest in it beyond our own life span. Except for a handful of historians, anthropologists, and ecologists, we are oblivious to how dramatically our lives differ from those of the 19th and even 20th century, let alone since the origins of *Homo sapiens*. Our grasp of time is honed in on minutes, hours, days, and months. For periods much shorter or longer (for example, milliseconds or centuries), we find them harder to cope with or plan. We evolved to think in terms of ourselves, our kin, and immediate descendants.

Our DNA, coding for our brains as well as our backs, was worked out in the rigors of 30–40 year survival tests. Reproduction especially wasn't relevant beyond such periods, so presumably the brains and behavioral propensities of elders had little effect on the human genotype. There would have been little selective advantage to long-functioning minds when long-functioning bodies weren't in the cards. Even today, only the rarest of humans pass on their genes past the age of 55 (perhaps 60 for men and 50 for women). Today's lifespans of 60, 80, or 100 years—replete with retirements and pensions—are very new to the human experience. The effects of these long lives on brain evolution would be indirect at best; perhaps, for example, with older political leadership having selective effects on the success of younger classes and cultures. Even these indirect effects could hardly have played out yet to a significant degree, as very long lifespans are so recent to the human scene. As it stands now, then, the senility of our eldest seems almost fitting in cultures obsessed (as they naturally are) with youthful and short-term pursuits, because the thoughts of such elders become less relevant in a direct, evolutionary sense.

Modern individuals pursuing short-term goals, often involving money or power, have an easier time achieving them than people with long-term goals because the gratification for achieving a short-term goal occurs more quickly than reaching a long-term one. Assisted not only by our own evolved propensities, but by neoclassical economists, we quite literally "discount" the future. The virtue of waiting, saving, and tempering our plans is undervalued and underfunded.

The factors above—sensory and evolutionary factors—may help us understand why few people show much interest in the future beyond the next few years. Some people have longer-term interests in certain aspects of the future such as medicine, aviation, communications, weaponry, education, or their own retirement. Very few have more than a cursory interest in the long-term, big picture, such as what our lives and our planet will be like 20, 50, or 500 years from now. This lack of interest and concern leaves our planet and future generations with few protectors in these dangerous times.

While we as individuals often plan for the very near future, and understandably so, even governments, corporations, and non-profit organizations generally ignore what might happen more than five years ahead. I once helped a large and well-known hospital in Chicago with "master planning." The hospital had added a few wings and assumed additional growth would never be required. Not many years later, another expansion was needed, and the earlier lack of foresight made for an awkward and expensive expansion project. Similarly, a retirement community I'm familiar with spent a million dollars building a garden for its residents. Just a few years later management destroyed it to make room for more assisted living facilities! It is hard for many of us to understand that life, society, and institutions can go through momentous changes in a matter of a few years, and it's even harder for us to plan for these changes.

How We Do Think

Evolution brought us to a system of decision-making that largely circumvents the need for logic. Our everyday thinking most often bypasses logic and depends to a large extent on referring back to what we already know (or think we know). I observe this thought process in myself. If I want to go from point A to point B as I have a number of times before, I do not analyze my route for efficiency, pleasantness, or even changes in conditions. I just follow the path I've used before.

Similarly, when I meet someone I don't know, in order to be able to interact with them quickly, I rely on formalities my mind has previously constructed. These formalities could be asking the person's name, occupation, or where they're from. I've asked these questions a thousand times before; they require no original thought on my part. My subconscious guides me. Unfortunately, when we just go through the motions, carrying on the same way every day without evaluating our actions, we are left with important shortcomings in the way we deal with reality.

What we already know, believe, or suspect largely determines the information we use in our thinking processes. Many people have a great attraction to ideas that have no grounding in fact whatsoever. We often favor ideas that are based instead on familiarity or presumption if not superstition, biases, and political or religious agendas. (In nearly a century of life in America, I've

SPOTLIGHT 3.1: Global Population Growth

Growth in human population sets the past century apart from all previous human history. Before 1900, no human generations had seen increases in human population like the ones experienced between 1900 and 2013, when the human family increased nearly fivefold. The tremendous acceleration of human population growth is sometimes illustrated by showing the quickening pace at which population has reached various billion-person landmarks. That perspective is reflected in Figure 10.

For thousands of human generations who lived as hunter-gatherers or in small villages or towns, the idea of a billion-person world would have seemed fantastical. By contrast, the generation born just before 1927—today's 94-year-olds and older—has lived through five separate billion-person additions to the global population, an unprecedented demographic acceleration. Indeed, most of us experience today's rapid population growth as yawningly normal: We hardly notice that humanity compresses into about a decade—the same population increase that occurred between the Stone Age and the Industrial Revolution.

Figure 10 also shows that global population growth has begun to slow a bit, and the period between billion-person additions is projected to lengthen slightly in the decades ahead. But the locomotive-like momentum of population growth means that billions more are likely to be added before global population stabilizes: Humans numbered 7.1 billion in 2014 but are projected to reach 10 billion around 2060, and the United Nations does not project a peak in global population until after 2100 (data cited here are based on the UN's "medium variant" projections, a middle estimate of population growth).

While the global trend is strongly upward for decades ahead, most of this growth will occur in developing countries as improvements in public health lower mortality rates there (See Figure 11). Already, 95 percent of the global increase in population occurs in developing countries, and this share is projected to grow over the rest of the century. By contrast, some industrial nations—Japan, Russia, and Germany are the largest of these—have recently begun to shrink in population, and China, the world's most populous country, is projected to see its population peak by around 2030, then start to contract. But growth in the developing world—again, largely because of a welcome decrease in mortality rates—is likely to more than offset these notable declines, which is why global population continues to surge upward.

Figure 10. Global Population Landmarks. United Nations, 2013.

	Global Population Landmark (billion persons)	Year Landmark Reached	Years to Reach Landmark
Historical	1	1804	Tens of thousands
	2	1927	123
	3	1960	33
	4	1974	14
	5	1987	13
	6	1999	12
	7	2011	12
Future	8	~2025	14
	9	~2040	15
	10	~2060	20

Figure 11. Global Population Growth, Developing and Developed Countries. United Nations, 2013.

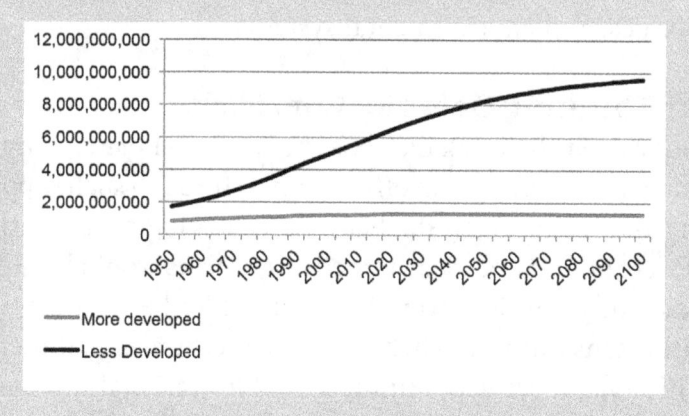

> **Literature Cited**
>
> "Historical Estimates of World Population," United States Census Bureau, last updated on July 5, 2018, https://www.census.gov/data/tables/time-series/demo/international-programs/historical-est-worldpop.html.
>
> "2019 Revision of World Population Prospects," Department of Economic and Social Affairs, United Nations, last updated on August 28, 2019, http://esa.un.org/unpd/wpp/unpp/panel_population.htm.

never seen a more extreme example than the "QAnon" conspiracy theory permeating far-right politics as this book goes to press.)

What if an acquaintance from your social and demographic peer group told you that a grocery store you favor has a rat infestation? You might stop going to that store altogether, without even verifying whether they have a rat problem or not, because the "informant" was from your in-group. Very quickly, biased "conclusions" become new "knowledge" and in turn distort new data selection and analysis. This process can open the door to trouble when dealing with reality, which includes complex problems such as those involving politics, international relations, economics, and environmental systems.

Clear Thinking Does Not Come Easy

We have self-flattering illusions about our ability to reason. We distinguish ourselves from other animals through such supposed ability, but reality suggests that we aren't as logical as we think. If we were honest and clearheaded, arguments would be quickly settled, and both sides would be grateful for becoming wiser.

Our brains evolved to help us survive as hunter-gatherers. In that lifestyle, there was a limited need for rational thought. In fact, when quick decisions were needed, spending time thinking things out could be dangerous. Imagine you're a hunter-gatherer, and you see a grizzly bear nearby. Do you stick around picking berries while you think about what to do, or do you immediately seek cover?

Even today we gravitate toward quick, easily understood solutions. Our fast-paced world has further normalized us to want to consume information quickly and efficiently, typically not even taking the time to investigate its accuracy. If facts are not presented quickly and in obvious terms, we lose interest. Unfortunately, such heuristic thinking leaves us ill-prepared to deal with the complexities and dangers of the world we now live in. We have not learned to curb the devastating effects we are leaving on our planet; the solutions are not simple and quick.

The struggle to be more rational is an arduous one because of the natural irrationality that exists worldwide, involving most people, their governments, and their media. Skimping on worthwhile and crucial projects, nations spend huge amounts of money on armaments and hostilities. Or they focus on one disaster, ignoring the bigger picture of its cause.

In October 1988 the USA, Soviet Union, and 150 journalists spent nearly 6 million dollars to cover the story of three gray whales caught in a rapidly closing hole in the Arctic sea ice.[19] People around the world worried for the whales and monitored the situation daily. Unnoticed, during the same three-week period the world population increased by nearly 5,000,000 people and 500,000 thousand children died as a result of malnutrition. In fact, during the preceding (1987) whaling season, as many as 809 whales were commercially slaughtered with little public outcry.[20]

While logical thinking can be so elusive, and although many things remain a mystery, science has given us insights that help us better understand the universe, our planet, and ourselves. Nonetheless, in spite of considerable evidence, many people casually reject scientific findings. The popularity of astrology, pseudoscience, and conspiracy theories attests to this. Many individuals and powerful leaders refuse to consider scientific evidence, brushing it off as "fake news." We just cannot believe the evidence when it shows that we are headed for such extreme, disastrous outcomes.

Special interests have taken advantage of and promoted this skepticism for their own benefit. Rational public discussion of topics such as birth control and climate change becomes impossible. Information that implies the need for substantial behavioral adjustments can produce anxiety, so people may react with denial. Alternatively, they may place their blind faith in technology, or in charismatic politicians to figure out ways to deal with the problem without requiring any sacrifices.

For example, the right to family planning and abortion is under continual debate. There is little real discussion beyond the "right-to-lifers" claiming that abortion is murder and a sin, regardless of circumstances, and the pro-choice people asserting that women should have the right to choose. There is little objective debate about when a human life begins, or what kind of a life unwanted children will lead, much less the impact of our already burgeoning population.

Another example is when Republicans repeatedly clamor to keep taxes down for the rich in order to enable them to "create" jobs. They are not challenged by the media to explain how this system is supposed to work when workers are relentlessly laid off to save corporations money and increase CEO bonuses instead.

A trait psychologists call "motivated reasoning" impels us to cling to erroneous beliefs in spite of overwhelming evidence against such beliefs. Instead of objectively searching for accurate information that either confirms or dispels a particular belief, we tend to seek out information, true or false, that confirms what we already believe. This thought process is widespread and has a devastating effect on how we live on this planet. People who see climate change as threatening their way of life or their income embrace ideas, individuals, and corporations who deny that humanity has any effect on the planet.

Ignoring or distorting our view of reality becomes more

dangerous as our impact on the planet increases and our world becomes more complex. Our attraction to quick, easy, simplistic solutions to complex problems, and failure to think about their side effects, is pervasive. Working against our instincts and forcing ourselves to think deeper and harder—individually and on a societal level—could be the only way for us to wake ourselves up to the state of our planet.

Imagination

There are two ways we learn about the world beyond ourselves. Sensation, which tells us what is happening immediately and directly to our bodies, is far stronger than cognition, which tells us what is happening beyond ourselves. What we see and feel is stronger than what we learn secondhand from outside sources. The more imaginative we are, the better we are able to narrow this gap between sensation and cognition and gain a broader view of reality.

Imagination plays an important part in civil society. It allows us to empathize with other people. We can picture people in far-off places or in the future. We can visualize different possible futures and construct "what if" scenarios. We can put ourselves into the shoes of others. Imagination prompts us to extend our concern beyond ourselves.

Imagination varies greatly from person to person, but it seems to be far from adequate for the needs of today. Evidence and statistics indicate that in a few decades our world will be very different than it is today, yet it is very hard for most of us to imagine it clearly. Climate change and future water shortages do not arouse most people the way a current recession or tax increase does. Problems close at hand or similar to those we have already experienced are easy to comprehend; others are not. We see our current environment and wasteful lifestyle as the norm. Ignoring the fact that there are millions of starving people on this planet, for many of us it seems normal to drive fifteen miles to a shopping center or buy the newest toy as soon as it's released. Even vacationing at luxurious resorts seems mundane to many. With our lack of imagination, we've come to view such profligate consumption as "normal," even while it pulls out the rug from our kids and grandkids.

Compelling Primary Drives

We can only help so much of who we are. As a species that has been evolving and adapting to this planet for hundreds of thousands of years, we carry with us many of the primitive drives that used to ensure our survival and procreation. Though these traits might have served us faithfully as hunter-gatherers, they are inhibiting our ability to function as modern citizens in a time when we need big-picture, long-term thinking. Many of these traits are interconnected, and it can seem overwhelming to try to overcome them. But if we can gradually become aware of our innate flaws, we have a chance to compensate for them over time.

Competitiveness

Evolution favors immediate and short-term winners. During our evolution, people who successfully contended for food, shelter, mates, and other advantages produced more descendants than others. Competitiveness was thus reinforced and became an intrinsic trait of our species. We strengthen this quality today by further rewarding winners with money, respect, and fame. Highly skilled athletes, business tycoons, war heroes, and even some dictators are respected and admired (such as Atatürk and Tito were). Many of us value success more than personal qualities such as kindness, honesty, knowledge, and wisdom. Consequently, our society is highly competitive. This competitiveness spills into arguments and discussions where we are usually more interested in winning than in coming to a rational conclusion or learning something new. Arguments often end up as clannish shouting matches, each side trying to convince the other, without hearing what the other side has to say. Most of us are not very interested in truth; we like to win.

SPOTLIGHT 3.2: The Wealth Footprint

Not surprisingly, national Ecological Footprints come in a range of sizes. Wealthier countries tend to have larger footprints than developing countries. On a per capita basis, individuals in high-income countries have a greater footprint than people in low-income countries. Figure 12 shows the Ecological Footprint per person of various groups of countries, categorized by income, and the extent to which each group overshoots its biocapacity.

At the national level, ecological debt also comes in various sizes. Figure 13 shows the top fifteen ecological debtors in the world and reports their deficit as a share of biocapacity. Several countries with the highest levels of debt per unit of biocapacity are located in the Arab Gulf, where water scarcity is great and forest cover to absorb carbon emissions is lacking. But other countries, such as the USA, are in deficit largely because consumption levels are higher than their abundant resource endowment can support.

Some countries with ecological deficits import ecological goods and services to avoid drawing down their own natural capital. For example, a growing number of countries (such as Jordan, Italy, and Yemen) import "virtual" water, in the form of products and their processing. But given that most countries are in ecological deficit, it is impossible for all countries to use a trade strategy that accommodates their overconsumption and addresses their national deficits.

Figure 12. Global Ecological Footprint and Biocapacity. Global Footprint Network, 2008.

Country Group	Biocapacity (global hectares per person)	Ecological Footprint (global hectares per person)	Overshoot (global hectares per person)
High Income	3.1	6.1	-3.0
Middle Income	1.7	2.0	-0.2
Low Income	1.1	1.2	-0.1
WORLD	1.8	2.7	-0.9

Figure 13. The World's 15 Largest Ecological Debtors. Global Footprint Network, 2008.

	Ecological Footprint (global hectares per person)	Total Biocapacity (global hectares per person)	Ecological Deficit (global hectares per person)	Deficit as share of biocapacity (percent)
Singapore	5.3	0.0	(5.3)	30,000
Kuwait	6.3	0.4	(5.9)	1,500
Israel	4.8	0.3	(4.5)	1,400
South Korea	4.9	0.3	(4.5)	1,350
United Arab Emirates	10.7	0.8	(9.8)	1,200
Japan	4.7	0.6	(4.1)	700
Saudi Arabia	5.1	0.8	(4.3)	500
Netherlands	6.2	1.0	(5.2)	500
Belgium	8.0	1.3	(6.7)	500
Italy	5.0	1.1	(3.8)	340
Qatar	10.5	2.5	(8.0)	320
Switzerland	5.0	1.2	(3.8)	300
Macedonia TFYR	5.7	1.4	(4.2)	300
Spain	5.4	1.6	(3.8)	240
United States	8.0	3.9	(4.1)	110

Literature Cited

"Ecological Footprint," Global Footprint Network, accessed on September 28, 2020, https://www.footprintnetwork.org/our-work/ecological-footprint/.

Hoekstra, A. 2009. Water security of nations: how international trade affects national water scarcity and dependency. Pages 27-36 in Jones, J.A.A., T.G. Vardanian, and C. Hakopian (eds.). *NATO Science for Peace and Security.* Springer, Dordrecht, UK.

We see our personal prestige as dependent on winning.

While worldwide cooperation is now essential for resolving environmental problems, our drive to come out on top makes cooperation difficult. Most people and governments focus their concerns on their own nations and feel that making an effort beyond that is sacrificing their national sovereignty. The refusal of nations to collaborate has led to massive overfishing, vast deforestation, plunging biodiversity, and existentially threatening climate change.

Violence

While the damage we have inflicted on our planet was not initially intentional, historically, much of how we have dealt with other human beings was. Killing and warfare over territory, differing beliefs, and acts of revenge date back to the earliest human societies. William James wrote, "History is a bath of blood."[21] Religion, which many see as the source of human ethics and civility, can be polarizing and has often led people to terrible violence.

Figure 14. Dr. Fritz Klein, a doctor at the camp, stands amongst corpses in Mass Grave No. 3 at Bergen-Belsen concentration camp in Germany. © Imperial War Museum.

Many cities in Asia, Europe, Africa, and the New World

were walled to protect people from others, and some of our greatest technical innovations have been in weaponry and defenses. Slavery also existed in almost every civilization and society, including Sumer, ancient Egypt, ancient China, the Akkadian Empire, Assyria, ancient India, ancient Greece, the Roman Empire, the Islamic Caliphate, ancient Palestine, and the pre-Columbian civilizations of the Americas. Slaveholding was still practiced in some parts of the world through the 19th century, including, for example, in the USA, Russia, and Ethiopia.

Racial hatred has been a leading cause of mass destruction for millennia. We tend to think of historic examples, such as the Ottomans, who brutally tried to cleanse their country of Armenians. And, of course, we think of the concentration camps of World War II. Racial hatred still permeates our world today. In late 2019, new evidence exposed the Chinese government for implementing a cultural genocide of Muslims. The "re-education" camps in Xinjiang province are said to be holding one million Muslim minorities, some as young as the age of 16. The horrors of ethnic cleansing still linger under the surface of our society, stirring up further hatred and xenophobia even in countries that are considered culturally tolerant.[22]

So, can we say that the Germans, Japanese, Serbs, or Hutus are worse than the rest of us because of their genocidal pasts? Their particular circumstances led them to utilize—in atrocious ways—the same basic makeup found in each of us.

I am viewed by others as a very calm and peaceful man, but I see violence in myself. Although I was generally a peaceful child, at times I did cruel things like shooting birds with a BB gun, stepping on ants, and pulling the wings off flies for "fun" or to satisfy some sort of fascination. Today, when I hear of gross injustice or torture, my feelings are not limited to sympathy for the victims; rather, images of harsh revenge come to mind. Fortunately, civilizing forces have worked on me, to some extent at least, and my own sense of decency constrains violent urges.

The capacity for violence, regardless of intent, appears in many species from insects to humans. In our case, organized society is a system that has kept our violent tendencies somewhat under control. David Anderson, a Howard Hughes medical investigator, put it this way:

> We have these inborn tendencies to aggression that are hardwired into brain areas like the hypothalamus and the amygdala, but we learn through parenting and training to keep these in check and that is due to the... prefrontal cortex that exerts this conscious control to suppress aggressive impulses.[23]

So there is a system of balance present in our brains: Subconscious aggression and violence versus conscious logic and training. But which one is stronger? Which one do we "listen" to more often? Why? Is there anything we can do to cultivate a more peaceable mind?

There is a powerful inclination in human nature for the strong to take advantage of people in weaker positions than themselves: to maltreat the elderly, children, and employees, for men to brutalize women, etc. Anthony Storr, the noted English psychiatrist, wrote:

> It is clear that human beings possess a marked hereditary predisposition toward aggressive behavior which they share with other animals and which serves a number of positive functions. An animal has to be able to compete for whatever resources of food are available. Sexual selection is ensured by competition for mates. Animals which live in groups tend to establish hierarchies which reduce conflict between individuals.[24]

Consistent with Storr's observation, we are not unlike one of our closest relatives, the chimpanzees. Humans and chimps share 98 percent of their genes. Jane Goodall discovered that chimps, once assumed to be a peaceful species living blissful tropical lives, make vicious attacks on neighboring groups.[25] Our tendency toward violence lies deep within us, indeed.

The desire for revenge, a trait consistent with our innate aggression, was responsible for much violence in the past and still is. When we feel we have been wronged, our instinct is to take action and get even. In the Bible, the Old Testament is heavily laden with revenge. The subject of revenge has fostered great literary works, such as *Hamlet* and *The Count of Monte Cristo*, and it holds an important place in many tribal and modern societies today, adding to the difficulties of maintaining peace.

Figure 15. "The Hanging" by Jacques Callot, 1592–1635.
© Jacques Callot/Wellcome Library, London.

Every day the news media are filled with stories about conflict and violence. News about constructive actions is generally swept aside, making way for "juicier" stories about competition and brutality. Journalists, politicians, and businesspeople focus their attention on money, "success," competition, and power, rather than on cooperation, creating, nurturing, justice, and truth. We seem to be fascinated with conflict and ferocity!

While there is a small percentage of sociopaths out there, presumably the majority of the population does have a conscience and would greatly prefer peace to violence. It would seem we have no excuse for our acceptance of violence. Nonetheless, our propensity for violence is persistent and widespread.

In 1914 during World War I, the English poet Julian Grenfell wrote his mother, "I've never been so fit or nearly so happy in my life before: I adore the fighting and the continual interest which compensates for every disadvantage. I adore war; it is like a big picnic without the objectlessness of a picnic."[26] Seven months later, he was wounded and died.

Gustave Le Bon, the 19th and 20th century French psychologist and sociologist, noted, "Among the most savage members of the French Convention were to be found inoffensive citizens who, under ordinary circumstances, would have been peaceful notaries or virtuous magistrates."[27]

Figure 16. The Arc de Triomphe in Paris, erected to honor those who fought for France during the Napoleonic Wars. © Library of Congress.

A famous controlled experiment conducted by Philip Zimbardo and his colleagues at Stanford University revealed cruelty in normal, healthy U.S. male college students.[28] A group of 24 people were randomly divided into groups of "prisoners" and "guards." Suitable cells and uniforms were provided and the experiment was to last two weeks. Within a short time, the "guards" appeared to derive pleasure from insulting, threatening, and dehumanizing the "prisoners" who became depressed, anxious, passive, and self-deprecating. These feelings became so intense that the experiment was terminated after six days. Most distressing to the researchers was the ease with which "normal" young men could adopt sadistic behavior.

A key question is whether women have a kinder, more peaceable nature. While some evidence suggests that to be the case, women are clearly capable of ruthless aggression as well.

New York Times correspondent Nicholas Kristof came across secret Communist Party documents that attest to large-scale cannibalism in the Guangxi region of southern China during the Cultural Revolution. He describes one incident, stating:

> The first person to strip meat from the body of one school principal was the former girlfriend of the man's son; she wanted to show she had no sympathy for him and was just as 'red' as anybody else. At some high schools, students butchered and roasted their teachers and principals in the school courtyard and feasted on the meat to celebrate triumph over 'counterrevolutionaries.'[29]

Figure 17. Sawing of three homosexuals from a 15th-century print. This is a slow, painful means of execution, since as long as the brain is supplied with blood and oxygen, the victim does not die until the saw reaches the heart or lungs. © Wikimedia Commons.

While we normally contain ourselves, it seems there is no end to the brutality we are capable of. In the past, executions were not just a punishment for misdeeds but were used to inflict as much pain as possible on criminals. As Christians know well, the Romans used crucifixion as a means of execution. Spikes were often driven through hands and feet to hold the prisoner on the cross; hours or days would pass as the prisoner perished in terrible pain. During the Middle Ages, breaking on the wheel, squeezing in the iron maiden, immersion in freezing water, exposure to hungry rats, dismemberment, drawing and quartering, and sawing were used to inflict terror and excruciating pain during execution.

We can't wipe away the memory of violence from our human history, nor should we. Ignorance and repression are just as powerful of enemies to us, if not more so. We can use our past as a long, bloody but valuable lesson in what we don't want to carry into the future.

Avarice

People have a variety of interests that drive them to fit into society in different ways. Some just want to get by and will fit in wherever they can. Others have strong interests that steer them toward teaching, science, the military, working with people, public service, preparing food, engineering, business, art, or taking care of the sick or victims of a natural disaster. For some, the smell of money or power draws them to do whatever will help them obtain it, and others just want to win, to come out on top and beat the other guy. Often the most aggressive, competitive, and confrontational people are like this.

Some of these people achieve positions in occupations that make or sell a useful product, others in producing something harmful such as carcinogenic or fatty fast foods. Others engage in outright criminal activities such as drug dealing, money laundering, and even murder for hire. To gain political power, some people will sell themselves for campaign contributions.

In the USA, the CEOs of corporations doing harmful things—such as making soft drinks and promoting them in schools—are paid orders of magnitude more than teachers, scientists, and even Nobel Laureates. Why are they not seen for what they are: Individuals who harm others for personal benefit and material gain? To me this sounds like murder, or close to it, yet many people admire these CEOs for their money and position, while granting scarce esteem to those who dutifully serve their communities.

The people who collect our trash provide a most useful and essential occupation. Yet they're looked down upon by people who load their garbage bins with empty bottles and junk-food wrappers. Meanwhile the CEOs of the soft-drink and fast-food corporations are courted by politicians, who then loosen the advertising regulations while minimizing the garbage collector's wage.

Gaining economic or political power becomes a positive feedback loop because it brings on connections with yet more money and power. Those doing work they enjoy for the public good do not improve their position in the "game" and are left in a weaker position compared with those pursuing money or power. Think of our public school teachers, charged with the education of our children. They're constrained by curriculum, deadlines, quotas, and budget cuts. Meanwhile they're notoriously underpaid. This is despite the fact that they are some of the most educated members of our communities, meaning that most are still paying for their college and university educations.

Selfishness

Several times when I was in grammar school I found myself being driven around by a chauffeur in an expensive car. I must confess it made me feel special, better than those other people I saw out there on the streets. Recalling those moments, I now understand why so many wealthy people have no guilt over spending a vast amount of money on material items. It's because the very rich do not feel the pain of the poor. They separate themselves from those of lower classes and confine their personal relationships to one another. With their clubs, private schools, private jets, exclusive vacation spots, and all the rest, the wealthy stick with those who share their interests, concerns, and lifestyle.

Figure 18. A homeless woman sits on a street in Chicago.
© Peer Grimm/ dpa/Corbis.

Their interests are largely money itself, the means for acquiring it, how to spend it, other wealthy people, and political support for their values. Their success in gaining power and money gives them self-assuredness, arrogance, and the expectation that others should kowtow to them. Because of their financial success, many of them are convinced that they themselves have the best understanding of the "real world," and they ignore much of the knowledge and wisdom of those who know more.

The excessively wealthy are blind to the everyday issues that others face. Many if not most of them don't know what it means to have student loans, to clean your own house, to struggle to put food on the table, to hassle with public transportation, or to jostle for traction in a world where everything is stacked against people in low socioeconomic communities. The isolation of the upper classes only perpetuates their obliviousness and exacerbates the social divide. The wealthy are more likely to ignore the pleas of the less fortunate or the advice of people more directly in contact with current issues, including scientists studying climate change, sea-level rise, biodiversity loss, and "forever chemicals."

Figure 19. Fairfield Pond in the Hamptons is the home of billionaire Ira Rennert. This home, valued at $170-200 million, has 29 bedrooms, 39 bathrooms, a basketball court, two tennis courts, a bowling alley, and a $150,000 hot tub. © Wikimedia Commons.

Those at the top often smugly take pride in humanity's achievements, overlooking the fact that the vast majority of inventions and new ideas were the achievements of relatively few individuals laboring diligently in the research and development laboratories (and with plenty of failures as well). When is the last time we heard of a CEO coming up with a life-saving invention, or any invention for that matter?

Occasionally I receive a flyer in the mail from 20/20/20, a WonderWork charity program, telling me that a million of the blind children around the world could have their eyesight restored through a $300 surgery. I find it hard to understand how some people can enjoy staying in a hotel room that costs $1,000 a night or more while many children are left to lead a life of darkness, others to the struggles of cleft palate, and still others to intellectual disability due to lack of adequate nutrition.

Nevertheless, the affluent do love their money and do not

part with it easily. I have a friend who is a doctor and an uncle who owned an art gallery. Both complain that the hardest people to collect from are those with a lot of money. Studies bear this out. In the *Chronicle of Philanthropy*, researchers reported that:

> Middle-class Americans give a far bigger share of their discretionary income to charities than the wealthy. Households that earn $50,000 to $75,000 give an average of 7.6 percent of their discretionary income to charity, compared with an average of 4.2 percent for people who make $100,000 or more.[30]

The love of money drives some rich people well beyond stinginess. In a controlled experiment on honesty at UC Berkeley, researchers consistently found that upper-class participants were more likely than others to lie and cheat when gambling or negotiating. They also cut people off more when driving, and generally endorsed unethical behavior in the workplace.[31]

Vincent Teresa, convicted mobster turned informer, speaking of his dealings with "legitimate" businesspeople said: "People are greedy, especially businesspeople, and if there is a way to make a fast buck, they'll grab it." When he was selling stolen goods to discount houses, for example, he noted:

> The discount store owners were greedier than the mob. They'd buy all you could get them, no questions asked, whether it was men's and women's clothing, furs, television sets, appliances, or shoes. I could have sold them ten trailer loads of goods a day if I'd had them available, particularly around the Christmas holidays."[32]

Some money- or power-seeking individuals go even further. These include highly intelligent sociopaths who resort to any means to achieve their ends. In business, Kenneth Lay, Bernard

Ebbers, and Bernie Madoff come to mind; noteworthy in politics were Hitler, Stalin, Idi Amin, and Saddam Hussein.

Belief

Beliefs are essential for us to effectively interact with the world and with each other. They motivate us and teach us to have confidence in others and ourselves. On the other hand, beliefs can blind us to facts, especially complicated environmental facts not readily seen with the naked eye.

When we only rely on what we observe or what we feel deep in our hearts to be true, our models of the world are woefully incomplete. For instance, we might still believe that the earth is flat (and some still do!) if we did not believe what scholars have told us. History would be meaningless—and so would science, unless we had conducted the research ourselves.

As evolutionarily driven people, we want simple, satisfying explanations for what is happening to and around us. For some, not knowing is terrifying. Without simple explanations for significant events, we lack a consistent foundation for our behavior. To satisfy this need for simplicity, we believe and accept many things as true with or without evidence.

When we cannot literally observe a link between data, our desire for an explanation compels us to invent a fictitious one, bizarre as it may be, and despite potential consequences. In his book *The Improbable Machine*, Jeremy Campbell noted, "We can turn nonsense into sense because that is the way the brain has been designed for a world where a fast, plausible interpretation is often better than a slow, certain one."[33] Although we often lack the curiosity, or don't want to make the effort to look at the facts, we tenaciously hold onto unfounded beliefs, and let them guide our lives.

Two thousand years ago, Julius Caesar wrote, "Men willingly believe what they wish." But does what we wish for stem from real, tangible evidence? Or is it from what our peers, parents, and charismatic leaders proclaim? Or what an institution projects? Or, simply, from our own emotional needs? In short, if we're not actively creating our own set of beliefs, then who is?

Our minds are influenced by our political and religious agendas and the groups we belong to. It matters a lot to us to have a belief that fits in with our group; holding a position that is at odds with our peers on a controversial subject can make life difficult. Consequently, it makes sense for people to pay attention to "getting it right" relative to their peers. Just as birds of a feather flock together, people prefer the company of those whose belief systems are similar to their own. It reduces social friction and some types of cognitive dissonance. However, similarly to the insulation of the upper classes from the rest of society, it also minimizes people's opportunity to examine new and contrary information that may lead to reassessment of their beliefs and widen their outlook.

When times are stressful, people look for security and answers, and they are vulnerable to demagogues with simplistic answers to their problems. Their vulnerability leads them to fall back on their in-groups, who may be run by these same fomenters, and blame the out-groups and individuals different than themselves; they can then become fodder for fanatical groups like the Nazis or extreme religious organizations such as some Christian fundamentalists or Wahhabi Muslims. Storr emphasizes:

> We may imagine that so-called normal people could never believe in anything so ludicrous as the delusional systems of the insane, yet historical evidence suggests the opposite. Whole societies have been persuaded without much difficulty to accept the most absurd calumnies about minority groups portrayed as enemies of the majority.[34]

We have a strong force within us that tells us that what we believe is right and rational. Few people question their religious beliefs or their social and political convictions even though most of the world's people think differently from one another. This stubbornness prevents us from questioning, thinking, and delving into a reality we shut ourselves off from, one where our planet suffers environmental harm every day.

Many people recognize that there are environmental problems, however, they believe that these issues are unrelated to economic growth, and that we can manage to live with eight, ten, or even fifteen billion well-fed people on the planet. Even if they accept that climate change is occurring, they believe that measures such as building floodwalls along coastal areas will solve the problem without requiring them to reduce their energy usage or change their consumerist lifestyles.

When the effects of environmental degradation become widespread and food and water supplies become critical, many individuals simply believe that we will be able to quickly turn things around instead of taking responsibility for their unsustainable economic activity. They think, "We have always managed to overcome problems in the past, and we will continue to do so." Some religious believers say these hardships are God's will, and we should accept them. It's easier for many to believe that power and control over the earth is out of their hands.

Ironically, many people see science like a religion, as a matter of belief. Disregarding evidence, a sizeable percentage of Americans simply don't believe in evolution, that humans contribute to climate change, or that biodiversity is plummeting. They want to believe that "there is no conflict between growing the economy and protecting the environment," despite all the science to the contrary.

Religious and political agendas often preempt reality. As psychologist Leon Festinger lamented, "... A man with a conviction is a hard man to change. Tell him you disagree and he turns away. Show him facts or figures and he questions your sources. Appeal to logic and he fails to see your point."[35]

When people are confronted with information on something of importance that they can affect, some will be stirred up and respond as best they can. Others will be informed, but do little or nothing. The evolved penchant of the human brain to overlook big-picture, long-term crises appears to play a major role in determining the proportion of those who respond.

In 1941 it took the bombing of Pearl Harbor to awaken Americans to the dangers they were facing. Our county virtually turned on a dime and set out to fight the Axis powers. Today serious environmental threats are here, but because they do not happen suddenly, and not always even visibly, they arouse few people. Nor do they affect all people equally—the wealthy and decision-makers who could take action are affected the least and last. Meanwhile, the media continue to focus on issues such as the economy, politics, and abrupt disasters like floods and earthquakes. As long as this is the case, environmental apathy will reign.

Chapter Four

The Psychology of Our Modern Society

Working together should enable us to resolve a broad range of problems better than individuals working independently, yet it often doesn't seem to work out that way. Despite the additional knowledge, talent, and ideas available in groups, countervailing phenomena interfere, including groupthink and bureaucracy. Rational, responsible behavior becomes even more difficult than it is at the individual level, and when we attempt to work together on a large scale as in a democratic government, decisions can be difficult to enact and original intentions of betterment or reform are sometimes perverted.

Social Psychology

Some years ago I attended a weekend workshop run by a sociologist friend. At the start we attendees were divided into groups and told to organize ourselves. We were told that we would then be interacting with the other organized groups. With much ado and jockeying for power, we elected officers and created position titles for others in the group. I wanted to discuss our purposes and goals, but in the scramble for organizing the hierarchy, titles, and rules of governance, my suggestion aroused no interest whatsoever.

Near the end of the weekend, we were told that we would soon start interacting with the other groups. Immediately our discussion turned to how we could protect ourselves, outmaneuver, and even overpower those groups. My friend the sociologist had never suggested that conflict or competition was a goal for these interactions—this behavior just sprang up from deep within us. We were not interested in the purpose of our interactions; we just wanted to prevail over the other groups.

Such behavior is well known to social psychologists. In 1954 Muzafer Sherif conducted his famous two-week Robber's Cave experiment. Twenty-two psychologically normal eleven- and twelve-year-old boys were brought to a summer camp setting where they were split into two groups. In the first phase of the experiment, the groups were separated, while members of each respective group got to know each other. Social norms developed, leadership structure emerged, and the boys became emotionally attached to their own groups.

In the second phase, the groups were asked to compete against one another in a series of contests. This quickly led to conflicts, including the raiding of each other's cabins. Rivalries formed quickly.

In the third phase, the groups were brought together and given tasks to perform. These tasks forced the boys to cooperate with each other, at least within their own groups. When the experiment was drawing to a close, the boys were asked to describe the characteristics of each group. They rated their own group favorably and the others unfavorably.[36]

The Robber's Cave experiment echoed William Golding's *Lord of the Flies* (also a product of 1954). In Golding's tale, a British plane crashes on a remote Pacific Island, leaving a half dozen adolescent boys stranded and struggling for survival and order. Two groups were formed, leadership roles were established, and the groups became hostile and even violent toward each other. *Lord of the Flies* became an emblem of the conflict between the civilizing and power-mongering impulses of boys.[37]

These impulses are not just prepubescent irrational tendencies; they flow through adolescence and develop further yet in adulthood. There are numerous other impulses as well, some of which are quite conflicting with others. Such impulses manifest in our interpersonal reactions—the way we act, think, or speak a certain way to others—and form the basis of social psychology.

Groupthink

Belonging to groups that share our values, beliefs, and agendas offers security. Independent thinking tends to cause trouble for people in such groups; it's easier to keep our thoughts aligned with the group's. Thinking and doing like others is a sort of psychological camouflage, lowering the odds of intellectual or emotional attack. Getting along in the group and joining the larger crowd rewards us with friends, and is the simplest way to get through life. Conformity, however, can also get us caught up in the hysteria of soccer-match riots, pilgrimage stampedes, or worse.

Figure 20. The Jonestown massacre, November 18, 1978, in which 918 people died. © David Hume, Kennerly/Getty.

Charismatic leaders can sway followers to perform atrocious acts, and because these followers finally feel as though they belong to a "family," they are insouciant of the trauma they are inflicting on themselves or others. On November 18, 1978, 918 members of the Peoples Temple cult died in Jonestown, Guyana, most of them taking their own lives pursuant to directions from their leader, Reverend James Warren "Jim" Jones.[38] Whether individual cultists were under specific influences of zealotry, drugs, or psychological manipulation, the whole episode was a case of groupthink in the extreme.

During the nascent stages of American democracy, founding fathers such as John Jay, James Madison, and even Thomas Jefferson felt slavery was an acceptable social arrangement. By then, slavery had been part of the "human deal" for 2,000 years. Pathways of slavery often wound through the more heinous territory of massacre and even genocide, as a century of Spanish conquest and conquistadors demonstrated.[39]

The prohibition of slavery wasn't the end of horrific groupthink. The Third Reich, for example, corresponded with one of the most educated and cultured nations of the early 20th century. Abolition in the Deutsch motherlands went all the way back to the Prussian state, yet the 20th century Weimar Republic was overrun by an anti-Semitic army of Nazis fueled by misguided and xenophobic rage.[40]

Figure 21. Germans giving a Nazi salute, with August Landmesser, who was married to a Jewish woman, refusing to do so. He paid for that.
© Wikimedia Commons.

When individuals belong to a powerful, passionate group, they can easily do things they would normally abhor. Christopher R. Browning, professor of history at Pacific Lutheran University, studied a battalion of 500 middle-aged, lower-middle-class men; reserve policemen from Hamburg who had recently been drafted and brought to Poland in 1942. Very few of them were racial fanatics or Nazis. On July 13 of that year, in the Polish village Józefów, they rounded up the Jews, selected several hundred as "work Jews," and shot the rest. They were not forced to do this and were given the chance to refuse. Twelve of the 500 did; the rest participated to varying degrees. During the 16 months following this massacre, they participated in the shooting of 38,000 Jews and the deportation of 45,000. After conducting many interviews years later, Browning concluded that the reason so few refused to participate had to do with career ambition and peer pressure. They did not want to lose face in front of their comrades.[41] As David Anderson of the Howard Hughes Medical Institute succinctly put it, "What happens in genocide is that it becomes socially acceptable for one group to do terrible things to another group."[42]

Now let us consider the commercial phalanx of "ordinary" businessmen and women promoting harmful products for profit and the intelligentsia of scientists willing to develop terrible weapons for tyrants. Even without the "excuse" of war, large numbers of people are willing to do almost anything if it is normalized and condoned by their peers. We take cues from people similar to ourselves so that we know how to act in a certain situation, but when the wrong or corrupt cues are given, it leads to a ripple effect of dangerous behaviors on a societal level.

This is what we humans are like, but fortunately with many individual exceptions! These exceptional individuals prove that, despite our own psychological deficits, we humans do in fact have an ability to control our primitive drives.

Societies Ignore, Too

In order to live sustainably we must deal with reality as it exists, not with some fantasy we might prefer. Although tradition is a stabilizing force in society, it often precludes the application of hard-earned, up-to-date common sense and sound science. Time moves on and we'll be in serious trouble if we do not recognize, acknowledge, discuss and safely manage the environmental dangers we face today. One would think that intelligent, reasonable people and governments would use logic to bypass fantasies and traditions, but all too often they do not.

There is plenty of evidence that we are headed toward an even more crowded world beset with shortages of healthy food and clean water. The future will be far worse as populations continue to grow, topsoils erode, aquifers are depleted, and fish catches decline, yet scientists and their data are ignored. Instead, most of us listen to economists and commentators who tell us what we want to hear. Influential political and religious leaders, too, cast aside what the scientists tell us about our environmental future, and they ignore the cultural norms and policies needed to mitigate these threats. These leaders are propping up a fantasy of a world that maintains their lifestyle preferences, pushing such preferences onto their constituents as well.

More than occasionally, I hear "energy experts" and economists discussing fossil fuels as if they will never run out. They also ignore the negative effects of fossil-fueled growth, including climate change. The belief that humans have no impact on Earth's climate is prevalent and profoundly out of touch with science, especially in the USA. A 2013 survey by *The Guardian* found that 97 percent of climate science authors agreed that climate change is man-made.[43] Nevertheless and nearly ten years later, American public opinion is split. Depending on how the question is posed, only 50–71 percent of Americans believe that climate change is caused by human economic activity. Among Republicans the range is 29–61 percent.[44]

Such confusion in the American mind, combined with the demand for cheap energy, makes it difficult for policymakers to pass any conservation measures. Meanwhile, without the support of the USA, climate diplomacy is severely limited.

What makes the climate challenge doubly disturbing is that information about climate change has been available for a very long time. In 1896, Swedish chemist Svante Arrhenius and, in 1899, American geologist T. C. Chamberlain, unbeknownst to one another, suggested that the burning of fossil fuels might increase global temperatures by increasing the level of carbon dioxide in the atmosphere.[45] In 1957, researchers at the Scripps Institute of Oceanography found that roughly half of the carbon dioxide released into the atmosphere stayed there. Humanity, they warned, was "engaged in a great geophysical experiment."[46] In 1965, a White House report to President Johnson devoted 23 of its 291 pages to atmospheric pollution. It warned that by the year 2000, carbon dioxide "may be sufficient to produce measurable and perhaps marked changes in climate, and will almost certainly cause significant changes in temperature and other properties of the stratosphere."[47] As a society, we still have not taken these warnings seriously!

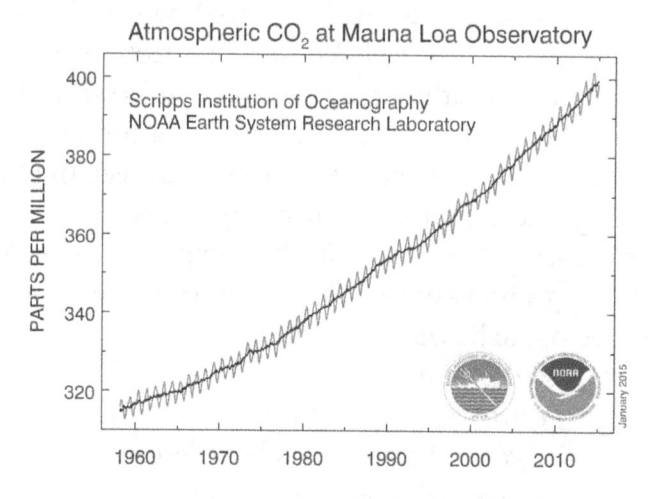

Figure 22. Monthly mean atmospheric carbon dioxide at Mauna Loa Observatory, Hawaii.
Source: "Monthly Average Mauna Loa CO2," Trends in Atmospheric Carbon Dioxide, Global Monitoring Laboratory, last updated September 9, 2020, https://www.esrl.noaa.gov/gmd/ccgg/trends/.

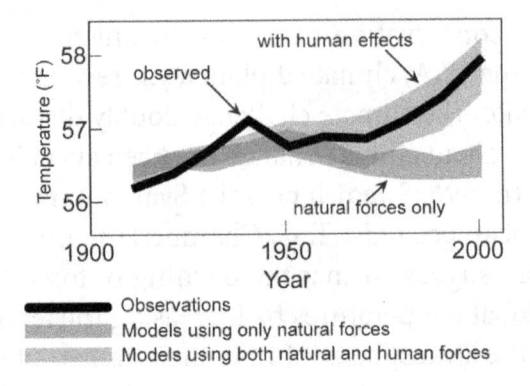

Figure 23. Natural and human influences on global temperature. Source: "Separating Human and Natural Influences on Climate," Global Climate Change Impacts in the United States: 2009 Report, U.S. Global Change Research Program, 2009, https://nca2009.globalchange.gov/separating-human-and-natural-influences-climate/index.html.

In 1948 ecologist Fairfield Osborn warned in his popular book *Our Plundered Planet*, "If we continue to disregard nature and its principles the days of our civilization are numbered."[48] He described the problems of overcrowding, soil depletion, and forest destruction. In that same year ornithologist William Voght's book *Road to Survival* appeared, which illuminated similar problems. The well-known intellectual and radio personality Clifton Fadiman noted, "*Road to Survival* should—and I think it will—arouse all Americans to a consciousness of how we are ruining the very soil beneath our feet and thereby committing suicide, not too slowly either. Let us hope it will energize a rescue squad, 140,000,000 strong."[49] Despite *Road to Survival* being a Book-of-the-Month-Club selection, Fadiman's hope turned out to be wishful thinking—and now there are 328 million of us in the USA.

Although we are doing some things to address environmental threats, our general response is best described as pathetic. The infrequent, shallow reporting on environmental matters fails to arouse public concern. The public's common sense isn't common enough without better media coverage. Politicians provide entirely insufficient environmental leadership for public education or media motivation. We as a whole are failing.

SPOTLIGHT 4.1: Today's Extinction Crisis

Biodiversity is the variety of life, from genes to ecosystems, and it is under severe threat by human population growth and economic activity. Cities and other human settlements have displaced wildlife habitats on a massive scale. Migration corridors and dispersal pathways have been eliminated or blocked.

The key principle is "competitive exclusion," whereby one species becomes more prominent by out-competing other species for resources. Essentially, non-human life comprises the "economy of nature," and as the human economy grows, natural resources are inevitably re-allocated from the economy of nature to the human economy, where the resources are converted into manufactured capital, consumer goods, and waste.

The re-allocation of natural resources from non-human species to the human economy has been a common theme of Earth's environment for approximately 2 million years. However, this process accelerated dramatically during the Industrial Revolution with the development of petroleum-fueled technology and the discovery of vast stocks of fossil fuels.

Most species endangerment and extinction today stems directly from fossil-fueled economic activity (such as agriculture, logging, mining, commercial fishing, manufacturing, and the long list of services that proliferate in cities), along with economic infrastructure (power lines, canals, etc.), pollution, and the international trade and interstate commerce that introduces invasive species into new, vulnerable ecosystems. With the global human population and economy at all-time high levels of production and consumption, it is no surprise that ecologists speak of the current biodiversity decline as the "Sixth Great Extinction." Rates of species endangerment and extinction are now orders of magnitude higher than background rates (that is, rates under typical ecological and evolutionary conditions).

A major development in our understanding of the conflict between economic growth and biodiversity conservation is the linkage of global warming to the growing, fossil-fueled economy. Climate change is a severe threat to species and ecological integrity because temperature is one of the most influential variables in the life histories of species. A relatively sudden shift in average temperature (say, within a few decades) has dramatic ecological effects, and the whole complex of climate change (which also includes sea-level rise and changes in precipitation, soil moisture, fire behavior, regularly reoccurring biological events, and many other ecological variables) threatens the unraveling of ecosystems as we know them.

Literature Cited

Czech, B., P.R. Krausman, and P.K. Devers. 2000. Economic associations among causes of species endangerment in the United States. *Bioscience* 50(7):593-601.

Czech, B. 2000. Economic growth as the limiting factor for wildlife conservation. *Wildlife Society Bulletin* 28(1):4-14.

Kingdon, J. 1993. *Self-Made Man: Human Evolution from Eden to Extinction?* John Wiley & Sons, New York.

Core Writing Team, Pachauri, R.K and A. Reisinger (eds.). 2007. *Climate Change 2007: Synthesis Report. Contribution of Working Groups I, II and III to the Fourth Assessment Report of the Intergovernmental Panel on Climate Change.* IPCC, Geneva, Switzerland.

We desperately need to recognize that the environment is at the core of our whole world—it *is* our world—and the stage upon which are played the comfortable lives we love so much.

Overload

If, as good citizens, we seriously concern ourselves not just with our children's education and personal needs, but with the needs of people starving in sub-Saharan Africa, human rights violations in Syria, drug cartels in Mexico, immigration and emigration, removal of Confederate statues, cruelty to animals, the welfare system, and "forever chemicals," we saddle ourselves with more than we can possibly deal with and risk becoming neurotic and ineffective. We are incapable of dealing with more than a few complex issues at a time, but we're also on the horns of a dilemma, because without public understanding and concern, solutions are not forthcoming. Our inability to care about and respond to a broad range of problems is unnerving, especially when the problems keep increasing in number and gravity.

It seems imperative to recognize the interconnectedness of problems—how they interact and affect each other. Perhaps then we can solve problems more efficiently, as if cutting a taproot rather than its many lateral roots. Unfortunately, the challenge doesn't end merely with recognizing interconnectedness; we still have to "chop the taproot" in our political and economic context—the political economy in other words—with all its corruption, bureaucracy, and general dysfunction.

Meanwhile the interconnectivity presents the public with more things to know and think about. Teachers have more to teach; journalists have more to report on; researchers have more to investigate. Much of it is too complex to explain in a nightly news feature, or even in a Sunday talk show. At the tip of the problem-solving spear, our civil servants are faced with more things to manage than politics will allow them to deal with in a reasonable way.

When the amount of relevant information is too large and the relationships too complex, the human brain selects, eliminates, and simplifies, sometimes down to a mere "tweet." But even with our mind's ability to filter input, we are still burdened with huge loads of data, much of it superfluous (like meaningless tweets in an expanding Twitter universe), and the rest of it hard to correlate and utilize. So, unless we are consistently reminded of big-picture situations such as biodiversity loss or ocean acidification, these issues fade from the public mind and politicians' agendas. Concerned individuals and advocacy organizations tend to direct their attention to no more than a handful of immediately pressing, narrowly focused problems, such as traffic congestion or lead in the water pipes, leaving the big-picture, long-term issues completely unaddressed.

Ethics and Values

In his book *The Story of the Human Body*, human evolutionary biologist Daniel E. Lieberman wrote, "We not only evolved to cooperate, innovate, communicate, and nurture, but also to cheat, steal, lie, and murder. The bottom line is that many human adaptations did not necessarily evolve to promote physical or mental well-being."[50]

Figure 24. Malnourished children, weakened by hunger.
© Cate Turton/ Department for International Development.

Of the many obstacles to responsible behavior we face, some of the most difficult to overcome are probably those involving ethics. Even when we discover how to solve serious problems, some people simply may not have the empathy required to bother. They simply may not care about the powerless or the future generations who have no way of defending themselves from our behavioral choices. These self-centered individuals, not held back by concerns beyond their own interests, can focus their efforts and energy on achieving their own ends. Altruistic individuals with broader concerns, on the other hand, spread their time and energy over larger, longer-term objectives, and lose out on professional, political, and financial gain.

SPOTLIGHT 4.2: Beyond the Numbers

Demography is much more than a numbers game: The social and economic variables that drive changes in population—including investments in public health, access to education and health care, and the extent of women's empowerment—translate to real changes in people's wellbeing. And changes in wellbeing, in turn, affect population growth.

The community of nations is making strong (though inadequate) efforts to reduce various dimensions of poverty, some of which could affect population growth. The Millennium Development Goals, objectives set by the United Nations for elimination of the most severe forms of human deprivation by 2015, have spurred action to reduce the number of people living in extreme poverty and cut in half the proportion of people without access to sanitary sources of drinking water. And major gains have been made in the fight against malaria and tuberculosis. Success in these areas could reduce death rates and therefore increase population pressure initially, but they are also likely to lay the groundwork for the economic and social stability that reduces birth rates and slows population growth.

To be sure, suffering is still widespread: Some 870 million people, roughly one in eight humans, live with chronic hunger, and some 2.8 billion people lack access to adequate sanitation, a major public health problem that contributes to increased death rates. And 6 million children still die each year before reaching their fifth birthday.

Meanwhile, the wealthiest in the world are extraordinarily rich. Credit Suisse's World Wealth Report 2013 reveals that more than two-thirds of the global population controls just 3 percent of global wealth, while the world's richest 0.7 percent of population controls 41 percent of the world's wealth (See Figure 25). Oxfam puts the numbers a different way, reporting in 2014 that the richest 85 people in the world have as much wealth as the poorest half of the world population, more than 3 billion people. And in all the high-income G20—the world's wealthiest 20 countries (except for South Korea)—inequality continues to increase.

Much work remains to be done before all people will have a

decent shot at a dignified life. Achieving social and economic stability will be a major contribution to dignified lives and stable populations.

Figure 25. World Wealth Report. Suisse Research Institute, 2013.

Household wealth	Share of world population in %	Share of world wealth in %
Less than $10,000	68.7	3.0
$10,000 - $100,000	22.9	13.7
$100,000 - $1 million	7.7	42.3
More than $1 million	0.7	41.0

Literature Cited

United Nations. 2013. *The Millennium Development Goals Report 2013*. United Nations, New York.

Keating, G. et al. 2013. *World Wealth Report 2013*. Credit Suisse Research Institute, Zurich, Switzerland.

Fuentes-Nieva, R. and N. Galasso. 2014. *Working for the Few: Political Capture and Economic Inequality.* Oxfam International, Oxford, UK.

Then there is the vast gulf of opportunity separating the fully fed and well-clothed, selfish or altruistic, from those living in dire need and desperation. Much of humanity accepts this divide and chooses to do nothing about it. Worse, there is evidence of veritable malevolence all around us.

Few remember why medicine containers are sealed to prevent individuals from tampering with drugs. While such sealing may resonate with common sense, the impetus was the "Chicago Tylenol Murders" of 1982. A never-caught killer laced over-the-counter Tylenol capsules with potassium cyanide, sending seven innocent people into frightening convulsions and death. Perhaps even more shockingly, this act of random evil "inspired" hundreds of copycat attacks in short order across the USA.[51]

Just as we can no longer purchase medications without tamper-proof lids, we cannot fly or enter a federal building without passing through security checks. Important politicians and many entertainers are protected by bodyguards. Security cameras are everywhere. We need virus and malware programs to protect our computers.

In the wake of catastrophes such as floods and hurricanes, looters appear to steal what they can from those already victimized and traumatized by disaster. In the midst of war-time misery, profiteers come out of the woodwork to take advantage of desperate victims while black-market arms dealers are busy selling their wares to hatemongers.

From my own observations, few of us are consistently trustworthy in our dealings with others. On the other hand, a number of us are outright crooks and about four percent are sociopaths.[52] Most of us fall somewhere in between these extremes. In *The Selfish Gene*, Richard Dawkins described how evolution maintains a balance between selfishness and altruism in the human population.[53] Those who lie and cheat have decided advantages of putting themselves first, while people more commonly look for and surround themselves with individuals they can trust, which benefits the honest. Unfortunately, evildoers, using tactics abhorred by well-intended people, can often overwhelm the efforts of those who promote peace, stability, and benevolence.

Religion and Other Beliefs

Many people see religion as the backbone of ethical behavior. That may be true; however, there are also highly ethical atheists, and some religious beliefs have led to intolerance, persecution, war, and terrorism. Today some people associate with Islamic terrorist organizations for the opportunity to spread violence, and believe they will be rewarded in heaven for doing so. In India, the world's largest democracy, peace breaks down along Hindu-Muslim lines. Not long ago, Protestant and Catholic zealots were killing each other in the Troubles of Northern Ireland. Ever since the war over the Golden Calf, some of the most ruthless wars endured by humanity were enacted in the name of God. Brutal torture was rampant during the Inquisition. Blaise Pascal wrote, "Men never do evil so completely and cheerfully as when they do it from religious conviction."[54]

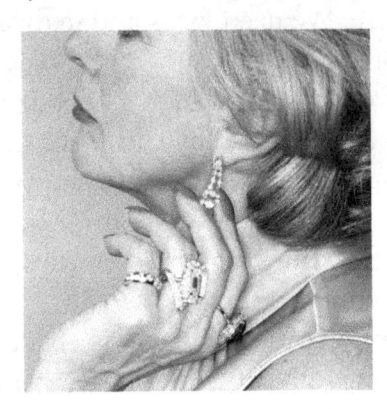

Figure 26. Enjoying some of the "better" things of life. © Kelvin Murray/Getty Images.

Environmental ethics are strongly influenced by religion, too. In the Old Testament (Genesis 2:28, King James Bible), God told Adam and Eve, "Be fruitful, and multiply, and replenish the earth, and subdue it: and have dominion over the fish of the sea, and over the fowl of the air, and over every living thing that moves upon the earth." This "cultural mandate" is viewed by some Jewish and Christian sects to apply to this day. Certainly it was applied *en masse* by Jews and Christians—and by Muslims, Hindus, and even Buddhists (and others)—throughout the centuries of their prominence.

Chief Seattle of the Suquamish Tribe evidently had a different point of view. He is reported to have said, "This we know—the earth does not belong to man; man belongs to the earth."[55] The Jains of India go even further. Besides refusing to eat animal products, some wear face masks to avoid breathing in and killing insects, and try not to step in puddles where unseen creatures might get squashed.[56] Unfortunately, such views are overwhelmed by the baser drives and beliefs of others. While we profess respect for the teachings of great religious and ethical leaders—Jesus, Gandhi, and the Dalai Lama among others—our pursuit of material goods, fostered by advertising, belies a deeper disrespect. It seems that God and ethics have been eclipsed by Madison Avenue and greed, with evil always in orbit.

Governmental and National Ethics

Aside from how they may end up looking in the history books, there are few incentives for politicians to care about what happens beyond the next five to ten years. Most of the unstated goals that drive a nation state are neither those of its most noble citizens nor even the higher aspirations of the common person. These unstated goals are more likely to be those of the politically crafty and financially advantaged, plus the most common and rudimentary demands of an unedified public. Whatever these goals may be, they become honorable and "patriotic" when they favor the homeland. We like this nationalistic outlook, for we can let loose our primitive impulses, get what we *think* we want, and be proud of ourselves as well as our country.

When our government says that it is acting "in the national interest," it is often just lending an ethical tone to what is simply selfishness. Supporting such action becomes solid citizenship. Questioning such activity is frowned upon and conducting government on an ethical basis can be suicide for a politician. Should a government conduct its international affairs on a strictly ethical basis, there would be a huge public outcry. Say for example there is a valuable resource—such as oil—that numerous nations want access to in order to thrive. Even if our country uses underhanded or aggressive tactics to get the oil, we see it as a victory over other countries. We become proud (and in many cases even boastful) of our country's success, and quickly ignore the unethical and underhanded methods that produced it. By ignoring the corrupt methods, we essentially endorse them.

We allow and even expect governments to do things we do not permit ourselves to do. War, for example, is essentially state-sponsored murder unless conducted strictly in self-defense. Yet it somehow becomes acceptable if simply in "the national interest." Such acceptance puts us on an extremely slippery slope; all sorts of aggression may be excused if the "national interest" is otherwise shortchanged.

For most people hypocrisy, lying, deceit, and clandestine operations carried out against other nations are seen as nasty yet necessary activities of governments and the people who run them. Corporations and special interest groups involved in international trade are constantly thumbing leaders to create processes, legislation, or terms of trade that favor them and disadvantage their overseas competitors. The din of low-grade manipulation morphs into an unethical *modus operandi*, if not a cornucopia for the corrupt.

As centers of wealth and power, governments are honey pots for the greedy. In attempts to counteract corruption and cheating, with limited success, governments have brought in rolls of bureaucratic red tape: rules, reviews, audits, investigations, procedural manuals, and no shortage of forms. Bureaucracy consumes a significant portion of a government's resources and talent, making it difficult for civil servants to perform their duties effectively and efficiently.

Hunger for power and resources coupled with our attraction to competition and conflict have fostered wars throughout history. The inevitable strife among growing populations in a world of diminishing natural resources, food and water shortage, climate change, and sea-level rise will surely be causing wars for generations to come.

Meanwhile the evolution of the human brain continues to enable both ethical and unethical behaviors. The coexistence of such behaviors was tolerable when weapons were primitive. Today, by contrast, we have weapons that can wipe out most life on Earth, an Earth already weakened by our bloating GDP. We are thoughtlessly and irresponsibly squeezing the future of our species and planet in our hands.

One of the great generals of the 20th century, Omar Bradley, was intimately familiar with decades of development in the art of warcraft. He ultimately lamented:

The world has achieved brilliance without conscience. Ours is a world of nuclear giants and ethical infants. We know more about war than we know about peace, more about killing than we know about living. We have grasped the mystery of the atom and rejected the Sermon on the Mount.[57]

Unintended Side Effects of Good Intentions

Ethical behavior, a good thing in itself, can cause more harm than good when undertaken with no consideration of big-picture, long-term challenges. We want to provide food and medicine to impoverished masses in less developed countries, but without providing them with family planning assistance as well, we are surely setting them up for even greater misery as food and water shortages become unsolvable along with the mix of environmental problems they face. We need to work at the root of the problem—overpopulation in this case—for our altruism to be effective.

We show little feeling or responsibility toward those we are bringing into this world that we are so drastically changing. We seem to feel some misplaced obligation to allow couples—in or out of wedlock—to have as many children as they can. Many of us are even willing to support those children, albeit meagerly, if their parents can't or won't. Yet how many of us sense an obligation to assure that these children will be raised by fairly treated, healthy, loving parents in a well-functioning environment? Not many of us, from what I've seen. Rather, we think very little about what the future holds for abused, unloved, uncared-for children as they grow up and produce yet more such children. It would be interesting, and sobering, to know how many unwanted children are born into this world because their parents had no access to family planning, and how this affects the growth rate of the world's population.

In addition to locating and helping the hungry, we should be paying much closer attention to where population growth rates are highest and therefore least sustainable. Family planning is needed—and often wanted and welcomed—in many of these areas. First it seems like we'll have to overcome our squeamishness in dealing with population issues. Domestic programs and international diplomacy toward population stabilization don't have to be unethical or distasteful, especially compared to burying our heads in the sand, which is guaranteed to solve not a thing.

Ethics in Business

My father found great pleasure first in selling, and later in tanning leather. He enjoyed his work, was not greedy, and liked the people he did business with. Enjoyment of the work drives much that is done in business, but money is another motive, and for some people it seems like the only motive. The opportunity to reap huge profits while beating "the other guy" attracts scores of Machiavellians into business, especially big business.

Being willing or even eager to backstab, brown-nose, cheat, bribe, and lie helps sociopaths climb corporate ladders. Even when operating pursuant to professional codes, the competitive nature of commerce, and the fear of failure drives businesspeople to the ethical margins. As the influence of business is far-reaching among supply chains, marketing, retailing, and consumer interactions, bad behavior in the business community has the effect of poisoning our society.

Bad ethics in big business reaches all the way up to the Pentagon. Major General Smedley Darlington Butler was at the time of his death the most decorated Marine in U.S. history. In 1935 he wrote *War Is a Racket*, an exposé of the profit motive behind warfare. His views were summarized in the socialist magazine *Common Sense*:

> I spent 33 years and four months in active military service and during that period I spent most of my time as a high-class muscle man for Big Business, for Wall Street and the bankers. . . . In short, I was

a racketeer, a gangster for capitalism. I helped make Mexico and especially Tampico safe for American oil interests in 1914. I helped make Haiti and Cuba a decent place for the National City Bank boys to collect revenues in. I helped in the raping of half a dozen Central American republics for the benefit of Wall Street. I helped purify Nicaragua for the International Banking House of Brown Brothers in 1902-1912. I brought light to the Dominican Republic for the American sugar interests in 1916. I helped make Honduras right for the American fruit companies in 1903. In China in 1927 I helped see to it that Standard Oil went on its way unmolested. Looking back on it, I might have given Al Capone a few hints. The best he could do was to operate his racket in three districts. I operated on three continents.[58]

A similar story was told by economist John Perkins in *Confessions of an Economic Hitman*. By cooking the books he helped U.S. intelligence agencies and multinational corporations blackmail and otherwise cajole foreign leaders into awarding lucrative contracts to American businesses and serving U.S. foreign policy. A big part of his job was ensuring GDP growth for all countries concerned and in defending GDP growth as the metric of national success.[59]

While I never had to deal with a bona fide economic hitman, as an architect I had to be constantly vigilant of contractors who tried to cut corners by skimping on materials, ignoring safety protocol, exaggerating labor costs, etc. The temptation to cut corners is as strong as, and in some ways equivalent to, the urge to increase profits. In bidding for jobs, sometimes contractors have to bid against others whom they know will try to underbid them, and whom they suspect of planning all the while to cut corners during construction. The dilemma of the ethical contractor is the need to provide honesty while competing against cost-cutting chiselers. More often than not, the unethical end up far richer, even when their work is inferior to that of their honest counterparts.

Figure 27. On April 14, 1994, seven executives from Big Tobacco defended their deadly products before a congressional subcommittee, raising their right hands and swearing that nicotine was not addictive. Their own company documents showed otherwise. Quoting William Campbell, president and CEO of Philip Morris USA: "I believe nicotine is not addictive." The same statement was subsequently made by other executives before television cameras. None were ever charged with perjury.
© John Duricka/AP.

Every year around the world, about 8 million people die of tobacco-related diseases.[60] An honest shareholder report of a major tobacco company might say something to the effect, "Last year was a good year; we made roughly $22,000 for every U.S. death that could statistically be attributed to our cigarettes. Fortunately, we were not held responsible for the medical costs of these deaths. They were paid by the victims themselves or by taxpayers via the government."

If you or I went out on the street and shot someone in cold blood, we would be sentenced to life in prison or possibly even executed. When the officers of a corporation, for the sake of increasing profit, dishonestly promote activities that lead to the painful deaths of thousands of people, they aren't even reprimanded. In fact, they are often rewarded with handsome salaries, respect, and status. It seems to me this is exactly the case, for example, with the managers of large American tobacco companies, their lobbyists, and their supporters in Congress. When the Seven Dwarves testified before Congress that tobacco was "not addictive," they weren't even charged with perjury, even though they had all seen internal reports demonstrating the addictiveness of nicotine.[61]

Today fossil fuel companies are behaving similarly by funding efforts to confuse the public about the role of greenhouse gas emissions in climate change. Their propaganda is playing a major role in delaying the mitigation of climate change, an existential threat to humankind. You have to wonder about their CEOs and boards of directors. Is money all that matters to these people? Don't they care about their own grandchildren? Cigarette company executives can at least tell their children not to smoke, but the grandchildren of oil company executives won't be able to escape a deteriorating planet.

Chapter Five

Changing our Minds

As I hope the preceding chapters have demonstrated, we humans have caused most of the daunting problems facing us today. We've caused these problems especially with our unbridled population growth and our intentional push for perpetual GDP growth. Now it's up to us to solve them as soon as possible.

We've been taking some positive steps already, such as monitoring and even mitigating various environmental threats, but our efforts are falling short, as conditions are worsening every year. Warnings from scientists, concerned citizens, and the few journalists who cover the big picture are ignored by most policy makers and governments.

Not that official warnings should even be required to evoke our response. A commonsense assessment of conditions around the world gives us plenty of information, with little commentary required. Hunger in Yemen, genocide in Darfur, civil war in Afghanistan, sea-level rise in Osaka, rainforest destruction in Brazil, extreme heat in California, boreal fires in Alaska, water conflicts along the Nile, plastic pollution of the oceans, nuclear proliferation in the Middle East, territorial disputes in the South China Sea, military buildup in the Caspian basin, a coronavirus pandemic, the staggering maldistribution of wealth within and among nations, and the expanding intersection of threats (such as hurricanes and sea-level rise at aging nuclear facilities in unstable regions) ... it's not rocket science to realize we're in trouble. Big-picture, long-term trouble, if not existential trouble.

Now, what do we do?

Not All Responses Succeed

Many people seem to harbor the notion that, "if" some of the environmental warnings we hear are correct, we can just roll up our sleeves, put our American know-how to work, and quickly "fix things." It's a bit like Captain Edward Smith's thinking, during the lone voyage of the Titanic, "If we *do* encounter icebergs, we can retrofit with a double hull and watertight bulkheads." Some fixes are far too big for such late dates. The real solution for Smith, who was warned of icebergs during the voyage, would have been a southerly route and a slower speed. These simple precautions were rejected, and the fate of the Titanic was sealed.[62]

Figure 28. Melting glaciers. © 9088 Images.

Even if we fully applied ourselves immediately with all the techno-fixes at our disposal, given the environmental damage already in the books, 22nd century Earth—a single lifetime away—will be far different from the one we know (not to mention the long-gone, pristine Earth of pre-industrial times). We've extinguished numerous species; many more are on the way out. CO2 is now at pre-human levels and still increasing rapidly, along with the other greenhouse gases including methane and nitrous oxide.[63] Glaciers and polar ice caps are melting; sea levels are rising. It is hard to know which species should be considered native and which are "invasive," as ecosystems are unravelling across the planet. Yet we haven't slowed down or changed course. We are acting like a collective Captain Smith, rejecting basic precautions with everything at stake, and at such a late date.

Hopefully we have learned, then, that business as usual is not the answer to these many problems we face. This could perhaps be the single greatest "action" we can take, or at least the most salient first step. We need to acknowledge, explicitly and with emphasis, that we cannot just leave it to the politicians, the scientists, and the titans of industry to get us out of this existential mess. We must do things differently; very differently. We must, above all else, intentionally and explicitly abandon the notion that economic growth is good. Economic growth, whether from increasing population or consumption, is the common denominator of the threats we face. We need an intellectual wake-up call that results in a concerted effort to move away from growth and toward a steady state economy instead.

While the odds seem stacked against us and our ill-adapted genome, who is to say we cannot change direction? Unlike other animals, we do have access to copious information and the capacity to plan. While we'll never have a pristine wilderness again, or a wild frontier to discover and settle, developing a precautionary approach now could very well preserve a decent chance of healthy and happy human lives on Earth far into the future. The challenge is for enough of us to get beyond the usual shallow thinking, contemplating what really matters in our lives, and what that implies for our behavior, as well as what we demand of our elected leaders.

Becoming More Than What We've Been

We cannot be blamed for being what we've been; that is, creatures that evolved to succeed as hunter-gatherers. We are no more responsible for the human genome than we are for sun spots or asteroids. However, in order to live happily or even safely in the environment we have so profoundly modified, we must come to grips with what we really are. We'll have to openly acknowledge that we have simply not evolved to deal with the big-picture, long-term problems we now face. We must make a collective decision to do *better*, to transcend evolution with our supposed sapience. We need—literally need for ourselves, our descendants, and even our peace of mind—to make a conscious and successful effort to restore our balance with nature. This will take strong new thinking, sincere concern for others, and serious commitment to principles of sustainability.

It will help to steer the ship of our fate in a more sustainable direction if we start recognizing and discussing the fact that those of us with tendencies toward conspicuous consumption, excessive preening, and ruthless competition are acting much like animals responding to basic instincts. Thorstein Veblen's *Theory of the Leisure Class* is as relevant to our Hummer-driving, McMansion building, fur-coat-wearing consumers as it was to the Rockefellers of the Gilded Age. Yet we all have some of these consuming, displaying, and competing tendencies. We must come to see these traits in ourselves and others for what they are: Animal instincts that, when allowed to run amuck, no longer fit with the overburdened environment. If the sapience of *Homo sapiens* can overcome one evolutionary hindrance, let us hope it's the hindrance of conspicuous consumption.

We need to understand not only what motivates us toward unsustainable behavior at the individual level, but how we interact in groups of all kinds. We should remain vigilant against surrendering to peer pressure and fads, much less getting caught up in the hysteria of fear- or war-mongering crowds. Our collective conscious mind has to take control over the unconscious; Freud's superego over the id.

We must rise above Ortega y Gasset's "mass man" who is perfectly satisfied with the status quo.[64] Rising above the status quo should be held up as the model of citizenship and what we might call "human patriotism." Those who go the extra mile to reduce their ecological footprint, to share with others, and to eschew the trappings of Madison Avenue should be respected and admired as exceptional human patriots. Respect and admiration will more than make up for any loss of attention to material display. Just as importantly, as described by Abraham Maslow in *Motivation and Personality*, others will be motivated to follow the lead of the respected and admired.[65]

Knowing How the Human Brain Works

To function effectively we need at least a rudimentary knowledge of how our brains work. The human brain is the tool we use in dealing with each other and our planet. We must figure out how to overcome its deficiencies and use it to cope more effectively with the big-picture, long-term problems we face today.

We cannot exchange our brains, but we can improve the way we use them. We can develop techniques and tools that supplement our brains, overcome their quirks, and enable us to do things we normally cannot. We already do this in many ways. We use writing to keep records, and telephones to talk farther than we can shout. Accounting, data banks, operations research, environmental impact studies, the internet, and orbiting satellites, when used effectively, can greatly extend our brains' capabilities. The scientific method, the systems approach, management systems, operations research, computers, brainstorming, and conflict resolution techniques expand the capacities of our minds. Finding and using more and better ways to do these things—and with more of a focus on the big-picture, long-term issues—should be a goal for all of us and something we expect from others.

All the while, though, we need to stay aware of our brains' weaknesses and limitations, so that we are modest about our abilities and ideas and are more open to possibilities to supplement and improve upon them. Although our ability to reason is limited, it is essential that we learn and do our best to resist having our thoughts manipulated by others including charismatic charlatans and propagandists. Educators must help us to develop such resistance. I can attest to the difference our educators can make. Ever since spending two weeks in primary school learning about propaganda and advertising, I have been conscious of mind manipulation and have resisted buying highly advertised products.

If we expect to overcome the primitive drives of our limited brains, we'll also need educators to do a better job of helping our students think rationally. As the neurologist Michael Gazzaniga pointed out, "... the quintessential human property of mind—rational processes—can occasionally override our more primitive beliefs. It isn't easy, but when it occurs, it represents our finest achievement."[66] Occasionally is not enough; we must strive to do it regularly.

Understanding Our Dependence on Nature

It is essential that we understand how our planet works and how we are threatening it. We citizens, through our elected politicians and our lifestyles, are responsible for our effects on the wellbeing of others and the planet. We must recognize that we are dependent on nature, which maintains the remarkably narrow range of environmental conditions that is safe for us.[67] Nature provides us with our necessities and, when it's not overloaded, protects us from dangerous chemicals. But nature is limited in its ability to support our demands. We need to study these limits and make them a centerpiece of our public dialogue.

Public dialogue, meanwhile, will only be useful if the information we discuss is correct. The scientific method is essential in producing such information. It requires systematic observation, measurement, and experimentation. Experimentation entails the formulation, testing, and modification of hypotheses as required, followed by more iterations of testing. While plenty is already known about what we must do—and stop doing—to protect the planet and posterity, science remains an important investment. Up-to-date science is like an insurance policy against the ravages of ignorance.

In the USA especially, we need to renew our respect for science, and reemphasize it in our schools. A basic understanding of science should be prioritized along with reading, writing, and arithmetic. Our citizens should understand what the scientific method is, and why it is essential for understanding what is happening to our planet.

Just as important as investing in science is actively protecting ourselves from misinformation. Claims such as "climate change has nothing to do with human activity" are a serious threat to humans at this point in history. These types of claims are promoted by political and commercial interests, and must be expected in a world of people with brains like ours, adapted to small-picture, short-term situations. We need to be constantly alert to hidden agendas, shoddy science, and conclusions stemming from mere anecdotes.

Advertisers and public relations specialists have powerful resources at their disposal: Big Money, Dark Money, access to much of our time, the effect of constant repetition, and sophisticated psychological techniques. They have the ability to bypass our better selves and appeal directly to our strong primitive instincts such as greed, fear, vanity, and our desire to please and impress our peers. They have Americans, especially, molded into dependable consumers, full of "consumer confidence" to meet the needs of businesses expanding their markets.

It seems a substantial amount of what we know and think about is in the hands of the marketers. We know a lot about the qualities of certain shampoos, faucets, video games, and pain relievers, at the expense of what our survival on this planet depends upon. As a citizen of the USA, I am somewhat embarrassed by this. As a culture and a country, I think we *should* be embarrassed by this. While embarrassment is not enjoyable, it is a powerful motivator.[68] (Either way, it would seem appropriate in this case.)

Getting Curious and Out of Denial

From my lengthy lifetime of observing people and interacting with them, I've found that most people have very little curiosity about things related to how the world works, and how it will look in the future. Many people don't like to think much at all beyond their favorite subjects. It requires effort and the risk that we may learn things that challenge our beliefs; it is much easier to watch TV or browse the internet than confront the issues.

The bigger the picture and the longer the term, the less curiosity we seem to have. And, it seems like our curiosity is more shortsighted by the day. This is astounding and alarming to me.

Is no one curious about how we would feed the 10 billion people the UN has projected will populate Earth by 2050?[69] (That's only 30 years away, which hardly seems far off to me.) Will these 10 billion people be eating healthy organic foods—vegetables and nuts and fish and meats—or purely Roundup-Ready soybeans and Bt corn and "meat" grown from stem cells in a laboratory? What about the aquifers to irrigate the soybeans and corn? And what if, due to rising temperatures, the grain belt is further north, in places like Nunavut and Siberia instead of Nebraska and Ukraine, without the soils to support it?

Is anyone curious about who the forecasters are at the UN? Do they have any background in ecology, ecological economics, or epidemiology? How did they get a job forecasting our global population without such background? Which countries pay their salaries? Who finances the campaigns of the politicians leading those countries?

Why do so many religious people clamor against abortion, while at the same time electing politicians that are obsessed with GDP growth? Doesn't the obsession with GDP growth amount to a type of abortion *en masse*? Isn't GDP growth causing our climate to spiral out of control, our ecosystems to unravel, and our biodiversity to plummet? Isn't the obsession with GDP like an abortion of entire generations of souls who will never find life because we destroyed the planet before they could enter it?

Basically, in other words, our curiosity needs piquing if we are to start addressing the big-picture, long-term problems. We cannot depend upon Wall Street, K Street, or Madison Avenue to pique it for us, at least not in the proper direction. We must pique our own curiosity independently of advertisers, politicians, and public relations professionals. We must help our fellow citizens to consider the important questions as well; important for the sakes of their own kids and grandkids. It is only our interest in such questions that will prompt a discussion of them in the media, in politics, and even in the churches.

Knowing the Right Things

What is the purpose for knowing anything? In an evolutionary sense, the purpose is survival. Zoologists and evolutionary ecologists describe animal behavior as one move after the next in a non-stop chess game of life and death: "Nature, red in tooth and claw," in the words of Tennyson. Non-human knowledge, then, is largely an encyclopedia of survival and reproduction.

Such is not the case with 21st century humans. We are swamped with information that has nothing to do with survival, and beset by ignorance of what survival even entails at this point in history. Our knowledge and interests are spent on sports, celebrities, stock markets, gossip, antiques, toys, technology, the Civil War, wines, and opera. We monitor our Twitter feeds, watch Netflix, and play video games. A few enlightened souls still read books, travel modestly, or take hikes out in nature. Meanwhile, the temperature is rising for all.

Where, for our own good and that of our species, should our interests lie today? I suggest the following basics: how to earn a living, manage our finances, raise a family, be good citizens, support our cultures, and keep our species and planet healthy. Most of us do fairly well on earning a living, less well on most of the others, and miserably on the last. This is largely because we are way behind on developing and maintaining big-picture, long-term knowledge.

Yet perhaps the time is coming soon when a particular hurricane, melted glacier, lost species, resource war, devastating oil spill, political revolution, or nuclear "dirty bomb" will bring our attention out of the Twitter feeds, Xboxes, and sports channels, and into the big-picture, long-term prospect. When it does, we'll want to know a thing or two about some of the following topics.

Bigger Role for Women

As noted in Chapter 3, women are not immune from *Homo sapiens'* worst instincts. Yet it cannot be seriously debated which gender has been responsible for most of the industrial insults heaped upon Earth as well as the vast majority of military attacks. The track record of men is thus far so poor that we could hardly do worse—and could conceivably do much better—with more of our political and economic affairs guided by women. For all we know, perhaps there is something about the y chromosome found only in men that links them more inextricably to aggressive, violent, and destructive behavior. At this stage, we have little to lose by striving for more women in leadership roles, if not a more feminine essence.

We have compelling evidence for big-picture, long-term thinking among women, as well as passionate defense of our environment. Rachel Carson, wildlife ecologist and author of *Silent Spring*, is often heralded as the mother of the environmental movement. She sacrificed a career with the US government and a pleasant retirement to fight the carcinogenic pesticide industry, all the way to her own death from cancer.[70] Lois Gibbs fought valiantly against toxic contamination at Love Canal, and helped revise national environmental regulations.[71] Erin Brockovich took on the behemoth energy corporation Pacific Gas & Electric in California, successfully suing them for their contamination of drinking water with their carcinogenic pollutant hexavalent chromium.[72]

We also have Jane Goodall, the primatologist and

conservationist, most famous for demonstrating the social and familial nature of chimpanzees, and the late Wangari Maathai, the Kenyan politician, activist, and Nobel Peace Prize winner who founded the tree-planting Green Belt Movement in Kenya.[73] In addition to these are many other well-known women from recent decades of environmental action including Vandana Shiva, Winona LaDuke, Sandra Steingraber, and Berta Cáceres.

Figure 29. Rachel Carson.
© U.S. Fish and Wildlife Service.

Is there a pattern here? Prior to Al Gore becoming synonymous with climate change through his 2006 documentary *An Inconvenient Truth*, and prior to Bill McKibben becoming a household name via his co-founding of the organization 350.org., those on the forefront of the movement to protect public health and our planetary ecosystem were largely women. Ecofeminist theory follows this phenomenon even deeper into the past. The contributions from women to environmental protection is probably not a coincidence, but rather a product of the role of women in society throughout history.

For time immemorial, women have taken on the position of life giver, caretaker, and nurturer in families and cultures. Being the gender that gives birth to and traditionally raises offspring, women may have an evolved instinct to protect children, family, and others in their community from harm. It has also been postulated that because women have been historically tasked with domestic chores such as procuring clean water, and gathering and growing food and resources for their families and tribes, women are more instinctively tied to and nurturing of the natural environment. They had to consider what the environment offered to sustain the growth and development of their young, and developed foresight in assessing threats to their descendants. This would logically help to explain why we have witnessed so many women throughout history battling against the threats of toxins, practicing the "precautionary principle" before it was named.

By contrast, there exists a historical pressure for men to be risk-takers who see potential threats as obstacles to conquer. As a result, with men at the helm of power for the preponderance of modern history, we have witnessed a reckless handling of the risks from known and potential toxicants and threats such as asbestos, radiation, pesticides, genetically modified organisms, plastic chemicals, and nanotechnology, and from potentially harmful actions such as overfishing, deforestation, and industrialization. While many scientifically valid reasons existed to proceed with caution before implementing a myriad of technological "innovations" that have had the potential for deleterious effects on humans and the biosphere, precaution in the name of public health and ecological sustainability has nearly always come second to economic concerns by men in leadership positions throughout the history of modern industrial civilization.

Certainly numerous men have been leaders in wilderness preservation, wildlife conservation, and environmental science: John Muir, Theodore Roosevelt, Aldo Leopold, David Brower, and Gaylord Nelson come quickly to mind. Yet in many cases such leadership was linked to adventure and the protection of recreational pursuits such as hunting and hiking. Seldom have such pursuits been at the forefront of women in environmental activism.

Ecofeminist scholars have raised the prospect that traditional hierarchical structures of male dominance, patriarchal religions, and crony capitalism factor into the imperilment of our planet and our unjust global society.[74] It stands to reason that more women in leadership roles throughout the world, especially women who embrace the traditional feminine approach of nurturing nature, could drastically alter our ecological trajectory. After all, there is a reason that Earth is called "Mother."

Big-Picture, Long-Term Studies

It is essential that we look at the big picture and see our planet not as a collection of independent pieces, but rather as a single entity made up of components that interrelate and interact with one another and change by the day. Environmental and economic problems are never isolated but are parts of a complex, interactive system originating in our past and extending far into our future. In order to cope with the increasing complexity of these problems, our citizens must have a much better understanding of them.

Starting with primary education in the public schools, we desperately need education and training on, about, and conducive to *big-picture, long-term thinking*. In our public schools today, natural sciences are lagging and the social sciences are heavily dominated by business, economics, and versions of history in which "progress" is reported through the pro-growth lens of the business and economics courses. If there is any part of the school system that perpetuates the fallacy of unlimited population and economic growth, it is precisely those courses. Such courses are not inherently evil; the subject matter is important. The problem rather is the failure to acknowledge limits to growth and account for big-picture, long-term problems such as biodiversity loss, climate change, and sea-level rise.

Arizona, Louisiana, and a growing number of other states—encouraged with "model legislation" from the U.S. Chamber of Commerce—require all high school students to take a course in "free enterprise."[75] Given the emphasis on free enterprise, the focus on profit in business courses, and the theory of perpetual growth in economics courses, it's little wonder our students graduate and elect politicians whose main claim to fame is

GDP growth. An extreme example of such politicians is Donald Trump (in office as this book goes to press). It's no coincidence that these same politicians—again with Trump as an extreme—are ignorant of climate, biodiversity, and other sciences, and even seem hostile to science and scientists. They reflect many of the tendencies described in the chapters above, most notably greed, corruption, competitiveness, obsession with "winning," and narrow-minded, short-term visions that allow only their own preconceived interpretations of reality.

What would we call the new, corrective courses that would help our students and citizens develop a better understanding of the big-picture, long-term issues? Why not "Big-Picture, Long-Term Studies?" There is nothing about the title that would act like a red flag to far-right conservatives on school boards (such as perhaps with "Ecological Studies" and "Evolutionary Biology"), nor is the title abstruse (as with "Anthropocene Studies"). Who would argue in knee-jerk fashion against thinking big picture and long term?

Of course, when the big picture and long term gets serious consideration, ecological and evolutionary thought is inevitable, allowing for dispassionate consideration of concepts such as the Anthropocene. Sometimes, sacrificing our pet phrases is worth it for purposes of peaceable advancement of concepts and awareness.

A Serious Role for Studying the Future

For big-picture, long-term thinking to help us steer ourselves in better directions, we need a clearer vision of the types of scenarios that could be visited upon future generations. If a future scenario is disastrous—and clearly communicated to the public—it should help motivate us to do what is necessary to avoid it. If, on the other hand, a future scenario is peaceable, fruitful, and healthy, we'd be motivated to do the things required to achieve it. We need, in other words, to be "studying the future" in order to make better decisions today.

The naming of this pursuit isn't as important as how it is

conducted and what it accomplishes, but naming has implications for the success of a new field or discipline. These implications can be unintended and unpredictable, yet momentous. Such implications are worth thinking about before setting forth with a new endeavor. In this case, "studying the future" sounds slightly oxymoronic, as we cannot literally observe something that hasn't arrived yet, but its meaning is clear at a glance. The same cannot be said for "future studies," which could easily confuse casual readers outside of the proper context. "Futures research" and "futures studies" are somewhat cumbersome, and "futurology" may be too easily cast as somewhat cultish, like an intellectual form of astrology. As with "big-picture, long-term studies," "studying the future" is crystal clear yet without the red flags that may be imagined by those out to find them. (Unfortunately, the phrase doesn't translate readily into a title for a college or university major, but it would certainly work as a course title.)

Studying the future has nothing in common with politically or ideologically envisioning the future. I've witnessed many forms of such envisioning in my lifetime. In addition to the nationalist, nativist, fascist, communist, capitalist, imperialist, and expansionist visions of notoriety in the 20th century, I've seen the influence of dystopian visions from left and right perspectives (such as George Orwell's *1984* and Ayn Rand's *Anthem*, respectively). I also witnessed an exciting but shrill wave of "futurism" in the arts. And of course we've had a science fiction genre in the literature since no later than Mary Shelley's *Frankenstein* (published in 1818). The best these visions did for us was help warn us of the troubles we humans can bring upon each other, should we become complacent. Some were the visions of madmen; others were mostly for entertainment purposes. None were serious studies of the future.

Rather, studying the future starts with a foundation of science—natural sciences such as physics, chemistry, biology, and ecology especially—and proceeds with extrapolation and modeling to assess what will be happening to our descendants' environment. In particular, what befalls them if we continue with business as usual, prioritizing GDP growth over environmental protection, public health, and peace? The leader in this type of modeling has been the Intergovernmental Panel on Climate Change (IPCC), which has forecasted greenhouse gas emissions, temperatures, and sea-level rise based upon numerous scenarios. The IPCC is clear that population and GDP growth are the two most crucial variables in the forcing of greenhouse gas emissions and climate change.[76] That alone should be a huge warning! Unfortunately, the IPCC is vastly outnumbered and overlooked in our profit-driven world of short-term thinking. This is why we need much more studying of the future, followed up by effective reporting, funded by governments and philanthropic foundations.

In studying the future, social sciences come into play as well. As predictive models are developed, numerous assumptions pertaining to technological and industrial methods, political trends, and international conflict can be modeled to "see" the big picture *in* the long term. Yet these models have little chance of reflecting future realities unless they are rigorously underpinned with the hard sciences. As they say, "Mother Nature bats last."

"A-Fiction" Literature

While studying the future is serious business, there is no reason to rule out the entertainment arts for purposes of helping us overcome our shortcomings. The science fiction genre has proven to be enormously popular and at times highly influential. I for one think there is a huge vacuum awaiting what we might call "a-fictional" futuristic literature. This type of literature would be neither entirely fictional nor non-fictional. Like sci-fi literature, it would entertain readers with futuristic settings and plots, but unlike sci-fi, these setting and plots would be based upon real, scientific studies of the future. Why wouldn't such literature be every bit as captivating as sci-fi? Or more so, given the real possibilities that our own kids and grandkids could be living out the stories?

Certainly there would be no shortage of subject matter. What happens to John Smith, Jane Doe, and others in the middle of the 22nd century? How do they make a living? What do they eat and how are they dressed? Are there any glaciers left on Earth? What are the animals and plants like? Are reptiles gradually replacing mammals? Are snakes growing to enormous proportions at the equator? Is there still a New Orleans? What about Florida? Has the USA come under the rule of a fascist dictator? Is there a Sino-Russian military alliance with Iran? Are there still nation states or has anarchy ensued? Are there electricity grids and transportation systems? Has *Homo sapiens* returned to feudal or tribal ways of living?

It seems to me that such questions would be prime fodder for a unique type of literature combining the natural sciences, anthropology, history, and drama. These a-fiction books could be as entertaining as any other genre. More importantly, they could conceivably make a difference in the course of world affairs.

Evidently there have been some attempts at roughly this type of genre in cinema, such as *The Day After Tomorrow* and *Waterworld*. However, it is my understanding that these were more along the lines of action/adventure films and did little to develop serious thinking about climate change, much less sociopolitical futures.

Noting the lack of serious futuristic thinking in the literature, I attempted myself to come up with an "a-fiction" book called *2145*.[77] I wrote it as an outcropping from this book, which of course has caused me to ponder frequently what the future might be like. I've never been a fiction writer, and "a-fiction" didn't come easily, either. I doubt it will be a bestseller, but I hope it inspires other authors to do better, and to base their futuristic dramas less on action and adventure, but rather on the fascinating—if disturbing—trends in our climate and environment, along with our sociological responses.

Educating Journalists

Journalists are a vital bridge between reality and the public. To do their job properly, they need a basic science background and a clear picture of reality in addition to the standard tools of the journalistic trade. Unfortunately, some journalists cross the line into entertainment. Media figures must sometimes be reminded that presenting a knowledgeable expert paired with someone representing a special interest is not "balanced reporting," but misleading and therefore bad journalism.

As climate change and other environmental problems become increasingly obvious and newsworthy, many journalists should be eager to learn about these topics. Conferences and workshops are extremely important venues for this type of education. A good precedent for interactive learning in tandem with media coverage is the Society of Environmental Journalists and their various conferences and workshops.

Foundations interested in the environment must see the value in having better-informed journalists committed to providing accurate information about the environment. They should be willing to fund such workshops generously.

Moving Toward a Steady State Economy

This book wouldn't be needed if it weren't for the relentless increase in human population and consumption. The growth of the human economy is the single biggest threat humans have ever faced. We are pulling the rug out from under our own feet, and from the feet of future generations.

Limits to growth doesn't seem like rocket science to me. I've watched the occurrence of limits to growth for almost a century. In the 1930s, as a boy, I was aware of World War II, with Germany's pursuit of "Lebensruam," or Living Room. In the 1940s I saw farmland start to disappear in my home state of Wisconsin. In the 1950s I saw a tremendous buildup of roads and factories around Milwaukee. Then there were the pollutants and endangered species of the 1960s, as I started to explore the USA and the world. From the 1970s I remember especially the

OPEC oil crisis and from the 1980s the ozone crisis, a bullet we humans narrowly dodged by banning CFCs. In the 1990s politicians started telling us there was no conflict between economic growth and environmental protection. Yet serious, widespread talk of climate change started the next decade, with the IPCC linking it back to economic growth. Incredibly, in 2016 only pro-growth politicians were on the presidential ballot in the USA, and we elected the most pro-growth president in history, Donald Trump.

I understand that there are economists and politicians who claim we can grow forever, but I don't understand how anyone takes them seriously. Economic growth—increasing population and consumption—is killing the planet and aborting our future generations. Why are we still pursuing it?

Common sense tells us that we have two basic alternatives to economic growth: decreasing the size of the economy and stabilizing the size of the economy. I've often wished the size of the economy was much smaller, such as it was in the 1950s or early 1960s, perhaps. We had less traffic, noise, stress, and certainly less pollution and other environmental damage. We had more open space to explore, and more wildlife to see. Those born in subsequent decades can never know what they missed, and we older folks cannot be proud of depriving them.

Yet I also realize that moving back to the GDP of those years entails the loss of jobs and a cultural readjustment in terms of the goods and services available. The solutions aren't easy, but we are only making matters worse by prioritizing GDP growth when we elect our politicians and set our economic policies. We need to strive instead for a steady state economy with stabilized population and consumption.

We also need to measure not just the economy, but environmental and human wellbeing using other indicators and metrics. These include the Genuine Progress Indicator, Living Planet Index, Human Development Index, Index of Sustainable Economic Welfare, and Gross National Happiness. Given a rigorous assessment of correlation and causality, we are likely to find that many of these important indicators of our health and welfare are declining not despite of a growing GDP, but because of it.

Reforming Economic Policies

Saving our planet for future generations isn't likely to happen without major policy changes. For example, how can we expect to achieve a steady state economy when we have laws, regulations, and institutions devoted to GDP growth? The Full and Sustainable Employment Act advocated by CASSE is a crucial starting point. This legislation would replace the Full Employment and Balanced Growth Act of 1978, which locked us into the pursuit of GDP growth ever since.

Replacing our central macroeconomic policy—and reorienting institutions such as the Federal Reserve System, Department of Commerce, and World Bank—will take tremendous political effort and savvy. It may take many decades. Meanwhile, though, there are plenty of policy reforms that can help in the transition to a steady state economy. The most obvious examples pertain to subsidies and taxes.

We need to eliminate subsidies for mining, logging, livestock grazing, and intensive, industrial-style agriculture. We also need to hold polluters in the extractive and industrial sectors accountable and liable for the environmental damages they cause. We need full funding for the agencies and programs that monitor extraction and pollution, and assistance with enforcement from our state and federal authorities. Such regulatory and fiscal discipline will not seem burdensome if we can shed our obsession with GDP growth. Instead, it will seem increasingly patriotic as the limits to growth become ever more evident.

Similarly, our tax policies should be viewed not as crippling to business but rather as protective of our families and future generations. We badly need a carbon tax to lower the rate of CO_2 emissions. We need a distance tax on international trade and interstate commerce to lessen the amount of pollution from transportation. We should pass luxury taxes in the personal vehicle, housing, and clothing sectors, in order to lower consumption on flagrantly unnecessary goods. A tax on securities trading would discourage speculation and hyperactivity in economic affairs.

Getting Political

Policy reform requires politicians. Politicians pass legislation and direct our government agencies to develop specific rules and regulations. They and their staff formulate the budgets and write the tax codes. They decide which governmental programs to fund, and which to ignore. They can also subvert agency missions or take liberties in redefining them. During the presidency of Ronald Reagan, for example, several agency missions (including those of the Army Corps of Engineers and the U.S. Forest Service) were reworded toward economic growth.

If big-picture, long-term thinking is to take root in government affairs, we'll need not only helpful policy ideas, but the politicians to enact and maintain them. These politicians will need at least a moderate background in the science behind limits to growth, because they will face intense opposition from the pro-growth establishment. They will have to be able to explain why limits to growth apply specifically to GDP (a key political metric), and why technological progress cannot overcome those limits. Otherwise they will have little chance of prevailing over the pro-growth rhetoric coming from the free-enterprise think tanks, Wall St., Madison Avenue, chambers of commerce, and growth-oriented bureaucrats.

It makes sense for big-picture politicians to focus at the national level, because national policies are the most influential when it comes to economic growth. The federal budget and the federal tax code are handled at the national level. The monetary authority is invariably at the national level, too, as with the Federal Reserve System in the USA. Trade policy is also a national concern.

The big-picture, long-term political thinker is likely to be a "fiscal conservative," a "progressive" with the tax code, and a "reformer" with monetary policy. This amounts to a unique political niche. It may be difficult to obtain the full support of a major political party with such an agenda, but that can be an advantage in areas where skepticism toward politicians is prevalent. Such skepticism has become widespread in many parts of the world, including the USA.

Particular policies and policy agendas are not the only reason for getting involved with politics. Another major reason is leadership: political, social, and cultural leadership. Getting elected is not always the most important objective. When a long-term thinker runs for political office, the campaign is a unique opportunity to raise public awareness about the absurdity of pushing for higher GDP in the 21st century.

For those new to politics, it may be more feasible to venture into politics at a local level. At the local level, the relative importance of public policy might be a little less than at the national level, while the emphasis on social leadership would be greater. Much of our cultural identity is established in local settings, including our consumption behavior. That's especially important because presumably a steady state economy could occur without a tremendous amount of policy reform. We could establish a steady state, in other words, largely from the demand side.

Going in the other direction from the national level, we have to acknowledge that a number of countries have been mired in abject poverty for long periods of time. Nigeria, Pakistan, Guyana, Bangladesh, Congo; countries such as these do still need economic growth. They need more GDP/capita, especially. And of course they also need population stabilization to allow for some recovery.

Therefore, we need steady-state principles in international diplomacy. In *Supply Shock*, Brian Czech called this "steady statesmanship."[78] The wealthiest countries need to moderate consumption and lessen their ecological footprint, leaving some room for the poorest countries. Wealthy countries should assist poor countries with a reasonable level of economic growth.

Supporting the Right Organizations

For reasons explained in chapters 3 and 4, big-picture, long-term thinking is almost unheard of in the corporate world and governmental organizations. Such thinking would almost have to start and spread from non-profit organizations. Unfortunately, it doesn't come easily to them, either.

Social justice organizations have ignored the limits to population and economic growth entirely. So have the big environmental organizations. The Nature Conservancy, Sierra Club, National Wildlife Federation, Natural Resources Defense Council, and World Wildlife Fund have been complicit in the rhetoric that "there is no conflict between growing the economy and protecting the environment." It seems like none of the other NGOs have done anything to refute such rhetoric, either. Defenders of Wildlife, the Audubon Society, Wilderness Society, Environmental Defense Fund, Union of Concerned Scientists, Friends of the Earth US . . . none of these have said anything about limits to growth or the need for a steady state economy. Together, these organizations have many millions of members.

Meanwhile, organizations such as the Center for the Advancement of the Steady State Economy, Post-Growth Institute, and Population Connection have labored with merely hundreds of members. These organizations deserve far more appreciation and more membership. They tell it like it is about limits to growth, based on sound science and common sense, and they warrant our respect and support.

Similarly, non-membership efforts such as Growthbusters, the Global Footprint Network, and the Population Media Center should receive far more support from those who really care about protecting the environment, maintaining the economy, and securing peace at home and abroad. Organizations such as these, along with the general degrowth movement in Europe, offer the biggest hope toward overcoming the small-picture, short-term thinking of our people and policy makers.

Keeping Our Hopes Up

Considering all the above, it's not easy to be optimistic and hopeful. Maybe we don't need to be both, though. Optimism is little more than complacent assumption, while hope is a deep, driving desire that moves us to act toward what is desired. Optimism is hardly helpful and can often be harmful, while hope is a profound virtue, often found with the likes of truth, justice, and compassion.

Could hope, too, have evolved as a human mental faculty? It does seem conceivable, but that is a topic for another author's book. What I know for sure is that it yet exists.

Unless we have passed some particularly momentous tipping point, unawares, our hopes are not misplaced. While humans may never again enjoy the spectacular Earth of old, by taking action soon we can save a lot of what's left. We can reduce our ecological footprint, share our resources fairly, and stop inciting wars. The fact that we can doesn't mean we will, but it means we can hope, which increases the chances we will.

We have scientists who understand climate change, biodiversity loss, and limits to growth. We have authors who warn us about the "resource wars" that stem from economic growth. We have individuals and organizations advocating the steady state economy. The human brain did not evolve to focus on the big-picture, long-term challenges daunting us in the 21st century. Yet evolution has allowed some space in the human mind to ponder such challenges and recognize solutions, starting with the reining in of our GDP.

Therein lies our hope.

Endnotes

1 "Methane: The Other Important Greenhouse Gas," Environmental Defense Fund, accessed on September 22, 2020, https://www.edf.org/climate/methane-other-important-greenhouse-gas.

2 "Be Fruitful and Multiply," The World Counts, accessed on September 22, 2020, https://www.theworldcounts.com/stories/How-Many-Babies-Are-Born-Each-Day; "Children: Reducing Mortality," World Health Organization, September 8, 2020, https://www.who.int/news-room/fact-sheets/detail/children-reducing-mortality; AgWeb Guest Editor. 2019. Our incredible vanishing farmland. *Farm Journal*, January 21, 2019; "Rainforest Facts," Rain-Tree Publishers, 2019, https://rain-tree.com/facts.htm.

3 Nelsen, A. 2019. EU 'outright dangerous' in its use of natural resources, says WWF. *The Guardian*, May 9, 2019.

4 Ehrlich, P. and J. Holdren. 1972. One-dimensional ecology. *Bulletin of the Atomic Scientists* 28(6):16, 18-27.

5 "UN Report: Nature's Dangerous Decline 'Unprecedented'; Species Extinction Rates 'Accelerating,'" Sustainable Development Goals, The United Nations, May 6, 2019, https://www.un.org/sustainabledevelopment/blog/2019/05/nature-decline-unprecedented-report/.

6 Watts, S. 2017. Global warming is putting the ocean's phytoplankton in danger. *Pacific Standard*, December 29, 2017.

7 "Ecological Footprint," Global Footprint Network, accessed on September 22, 2020, https://www.footprintnetwork.org/our-work/ecological-footprint/.

8 Lovett, R. 2011. What if the biggest solar storm on record

happened today? *National Geographic News*, March 2, 2011.

9 Hadhazy, A. 2009. A scary 13th: 20 years ago, Earth was blasted with a massive plume of solar plasma. *Scientific American*, March 13, 2009.

10 Csanyi, E., "Large Power Transformer Tailored to Customers' Specifications," Electrical Engineering Portal, December 30, 2013, https://electrical-engineering-portal.com/an-overview-of-large-power-transformer-lpt.

11 Lee, C. 2010. Obama, Medvedev sign START treaty. *Politico*, April 8, 2010.

12 Hansen, J. 2009. *Storms of My Grandchildren*. Bloomsbury Press, New York. See page 236.

13 "Children: Reducing Mortality," World Health Organization, September 8, 2020, https://www.who.int/news-room/fact-sheets/detail/children-reducing-mortality.

14 Pinker, S. 2011. *The Better Angels of Our Nature: Why Violence Has Declined*. The Penguin Group, New York.

15 Koshgarian, L. and A. Siddique, "Where Your Tax Dollar Was Spent in 2018," National Priorities Project, April 11, 2019, https://www.nationalpriorities.org/analysis/2019/tax-day-2019/where-your-tax-dollar-was-spent-2018/.

16 Ortega y Gasset, J. 1932. *The Revolt of The Masses*. W.W. Norton, New York. See page 90.

17 Wilson, E. 2012. *The Social Conquest of Earth*. Liverlight Publishing, New York. See page 7.

18 Wilson, E. 2002. *The Future of Life*. Alfred A. Knopf, New York. See page 40.

19 Thompson, A. 2012. Big miracle: the real rescue in images. *Live Science*, February 6, 2012.

20 "Total Catches," International Whaling Commission, accessed on September 22, 2020, https://iwc.int/total-catches.

21 James, W. 1910. The moral equivalent of war. *Popular Science Monthly* 77:400–410.

22 Editorial Board. 2020. How China corralled 1 million people into concentration camps. *Washington Post*, February 29, 2020.

23 *Charlie Rose Brain Series,* season 1, episode 8, "Negative Emotions." Aired June 4, 2010, on PBS.

24 Storr, A. 1992. *Human Destructiveness.* Ballatine Books, New York. See page 21.

25 Pinker, *The Better Angels of Our Nature: Why Violence Has Declined*, see page 37.

26 Storr, *Human Destructiveness,* see page 15.

27 Le Bon, G. 1960. *The Crowd.* Viking Press, New York. See page 26.

28 Haney, C., C. Banks, and P. Zimbardo. 1968. Interpersonal Dynamics in a Simulated Prison. *International Journal of Criminology and Psychology* 6:279-80.

29 Kristof, N. and S. WuDunn. 1994. *China Wakes.* Random House, New York. See page 73.

30 Gipple, E. and B. Gose. 2012. America's generosity divide. *The Chronicle of Philanthropy,* August 19, 2012.

31 Anwar, Y. 2012. Affluent people more likely to be scofflaws. *Greater Good Magazine,* February 28, 2012.

32 Teresa, V. and T. Renner. 1974. *My Life in the Mafia.* Fawcett Publications, Greenwich, CT. See pages 108 and 145.

33 Campbell, J. 1989. *The Improbable Machine: What the Upheavals in Artificial Intelligence Research Reveal About*

How the Mind Really Works. Simon & Schuster, New York. See page 233.

34 Storr, *Human Destructiveness*, see page 124.

35 Festinger, L. 1964. *When Prophecy Fails.* Harper & Row, New York. See page 3.

36 Perry, G. 2018. *The Lost Boys: Inside Muzafer Sherif's Robbers Cave Experiment.* Scribe Publications, Brunswick, Victoria, Australia.

37 Golding, W. 1954. *Lord of the Flies.* Faber and Faber, London.

38 Conroy, O. 2018. An apocalyptic cult, 900 dead: remembering the Jonestown massacre, 40 years on. *The Guardian,* November 17, 2018.

39 Micalizio, C. and the National Geographic Education Staff, "A History of Slavery in the United States," National Geographic: Resource Library, National Geographic, accessed on September 29, 2020, https://www.nationalgeographic.org/interactive/slavery-united-states/.

40 Rosenbaum, R. 2012. Revisiting the rise and fall of the Third Reich. *Smithsonian Magazine,* February 2012.

41 Browning, C. 1992. *Ordinary Men.* HarperCollins, New York.

42 *Charlie Rose Brain Series,* season 1, episode 8, "Negative Emotions." Aired June 4, 2010, on PBS.

43 Nuccitelli, D. 2013. Survey finds 97% of climate science papers agree warming is man-made. *The Guardian,* May 16, 2013.

44 "Do Most Americans Believe in Human-Caused Climate Change? It Depends on How You Ask," Annenberg Public Policy Center of the University of Pennsylvania, May 9, 2019, https://www.annenbergpublicpolicycenter.org/do-

most-americans-believe-human-caused-climate-change/.

45 Cronin, T. 2010. *Paleoclimates: Understanding Climate Change Past and Present.* Columbia University Press, New York.

46 President's Science Advisory Committee. 1965. *Restoring the Quality of Our Environment.* The White House, Washington, D.C., See pages 111-133.

47 Nuccitelli, D. 2015. Scientists warned the US president about global warming 50 years ago today. *The Guardian,* November 5, 2015.

48 Fairfield, O. 1948. *Our Plundered Planet.* Faber & Faber, London.

49 Vogt, W. 1948. *Road to Survival.* William Sloan Associates, New York. Quote appears on dust jacket of original edition.

50 Lieberman, D. 2013. *The Story of The Human Body: Evolution, Health, and Disease.* Pantheon Books, New York. See page 13.

51 Fletcher, D. 2009. A brief history of the Tylenol poisonings. *Time,* February 9, 2009.

52 Stout, M. 2005. *The Sociopath Next Door.* Broadway Books, New York. See page 8.

53 Richard D. 1989. *The Selfish Gene.* Oxford University Press, Oxford, England.

54 Pascal, B. 1995. *Pensées.* Penguin Classics, New York.

55 "Chief Seattle's Letter to All," California State University, Northridge, accessed on September 22, 2020, http://www.csun.edu/~vcpsy00h/seattle.htm.

56 George, N. 2005. Jain ascetics give it all up for their faith. *Los Angeles Times,* September 11, 2005.

57 Bradley, O., "Memorial Day Address" (speech,

Longmeadow, Massachusetts, 1948), Guideposts, https://www.guideposts.org/better-living/positive-living/positive-thinking/general-omar-bradleys-memorial-day-address.

58 Butler, S. 1935. *War is a Racket.* Round Table Press, Warwick, New York.

59 Perkins, J. 1992. *Confessions of an Economic Hitman.* Berrett-Koehler Publishers, San Francisco, CA.

60 "Tobacco," World Health Organization, May 27, 2020, https://www.who.int/news-room/fact-sheets/detail/tobacco.

61 Hilts, P. 1994. Tobacco chiefs say cigarettes aren't addictive. *New York Times,* April 15, 1994.

62 Borrull, B., "Discover 10 ways the Titanic could have avoided sinking or saved its passengers," History Totally Naked, April 13, 2019, https://historytotallynaked.com/2019/04/13/discover-10-ways-the-titanic-could-have-avoided-sinking-or-saved-its-passengers/.

63 Freedman, A. 2013. The last time CO_2 was this high, humans didn't exist. *Climate Central,* May 3, 2019; "Trends in atmospheric concentrations of CO_2 (ppm), CH_4 (ppb) and N_2O (ppb), between 1800 and 2017," European Environment Agency, November 27 2019, https://www.eea.europa.eu/data-and-maps/daviz/atmospheric-concentration-of-carbon-dioxide-5#tab-chart_6.

64 "José Ortega y Gasset," Stanford Encyclopedia of Philosophy, November 20, 2017, https://plato.stanford.edu/entries/gasset/.

65 Maslow, A. 1954. *Motivation and Personality.* Harper, New York.

66 Gazzaniga, M. 1994. *Nature's Mind: Biological Roots Of Thinking, Emotions, Sexuality, Language, And Intelligence.* Basic Books, New York.

67 Ward, P. D., and D. Brownlee. 2000. *Rare Earth: Why Complex Life is Uncommon in the Universe*. Springer, New York. See page 368.

68 Rivero, L. 2015. Shame and motivation to change: could the emotion we run from the fastest help us to be better people? *Psychology Today,* January 29, 2015.

69 "World population projected to reach 9.8 billion in 2050, and 11.2 billion in 2100," Department of Economic and Social Affairs, United Nations, June 21, 2017, https://www.un.org/development/desa/en/news/population/world-population-prospects-2017.html.

70 Leonard, J. 1964. Rachel Carson dies of cancer; 'silent spring' author was 56. *New York Times,* April 15, 1964.

71 "Lois Gibbs: 1990 Goldman Prize Recipient North America," The Goldman Environmental Prize, acessed on October 1, 2020, https://www.goldmanprize.org/recipient/lois-gibbs/.

72 "Erin Brokovich Biography," Biography, updated on April 12, 2019, https://www.biography.com/activist/erin-brockovich.

73 "About Jane," The Jane Goodall Institute, accessed on October 1, 2020, https://www.janegoodall.org/our-story/about-jane/; "Wangari Maathai," The Greenbelt Movement, accessed on October 1, 2020, https://www.greenbeltmovement.org/wangari-maathai.

74 Gaard, G. and L. Gruen. 1993. Ecofeminism: toward global justice and planetary health. *Society and Nature* 2:1–35.

75 "U.S. Chamber Releases 'Model Legislation' to Educate Youth on Free Enterprise System," U.S. Chamber of Commerce, August 3, 2011, https://www.uschamber.com/press-release/us-chamber-releases-%E2%80%98model-legislation%E2%80%99-educate-youth-free-enterprise-system.

76 Nakicenovic, N. et al. 2000. *Special Report on Emissions Scenarios for the Intergovernmental Panel on Climate Change*, Cambridge University Press, Cambridge, England.

77 My first attempt at this type of "a-fictional" literature was in 2009 when I published *2045*, which no longer seems far in the future!

78 Czech, B. 2013. *Supply Shock: Economic Growth at the Crossroads and the Steady State Solution.* New Society Publishers, Gabriola Island, British Columbia. See page 367.

Index

advertising, 24, 50, 75, 88
"a-fiction" literature, 98-99
Africa, 4, 11, 43, 68
Agent Orange, 20
agriculture
    as enabling human life, 11, 21
    harmful methods of, 5, 67, 102
Anderson, David, 45, 67
Arc de Triomphe, 47
architect, 6, 18, 79
Arrhenius, Svante, 65
avarice, 49
belief
    erroneous and blinding, 38, 54, 56-57
    systems, 55, 73
Better Angels of Our Nature, 24
Bible, 46, 74
biocapacity
    global ecological footprint, 16-17
    by income group, 41-42
biodiversity
    extinction of species, 67-68
    loss of, 43, 52, 56, 69, 91, 95, 96, 106
birth control, 38
Bradley, Omar, 76
brain
    anatomy of, 45
    functions, 56, 69, 76, 87-89, 106
    as a tool for interpretation, 54
    instincts of the primitive, 28, 30-32, 36
Browning, Christopher, R., 63
business
    businesspeople, 7, 9, 46, 53, 78

nature and influence of, 23, 53, 78, 95
Butler, Major General Smedley Darlington, 78
Caesar, Julius, 54
Callot, Jacques, 46
Campbell, Jeremy 54
Campbell, William, 80
capitalism, 15, 79, 94
carbon cycle, 29
carbon dioxide 2, 13, 16, 65
Carrington Event, 18
Chamberlain, T.C., 65
"Chicago Tylenol Murders," 72
Chief Seattle, 74
China, 11, 23, 35, 44, 48, 79, 84
Chronicle of Philanthropy, 53
clear thinking, 36-39
climate change
    as a result of burning fossil fuels, 12-13, 64-65, 67-68, 81
    ignorance of, 30, 38-39, 52, 56, 89, 93-95, 98-101
Cold War, 15, 20
common sense, 64, 66, 72, 101, 105
    Common Sense (magazine), 78
competitiveness, 40, 45, 46, 49, 60, 67, 78, 96
connections
    between most human issues, 5, 7
    political, 50
consumerism, 3
consumption, 5, 8, 15, 21, 41, 67, 85-86, 100-104
cooperation
    as a necessity for solving problems, 24, 43
    resistance to, 43, 46
corporations, 19, 23-24, 32, 38, 49, 50, 76, 79, 80, 92
corruption, 4, 23, 69, 76, 96
costs
    environmental, 4

of mitigation, 20
　　　of production, 4, 12, 19, 79
Credit Suisse's World Wealth Report, 71-72
cruelty, 47, 68
Cultural revolution, 48
Dalai Lama, 75
Dawkins, Richard, 73
denial, 38, 90
dependence
　　　on electricity, 15-19
　　　on nature, 88-90
disconnection, 3-5
Easter Island, 11
ecological footprint, 15-17, 30, 41-42, 87, 104, 106
ecological debtors, 16, 41-42
economic growth
　　　as a tool for political advancement, 7, 103
　　　economic policies pertaining to, 9, 95, 101, 103-105
　　　in conflict with environmental protection, 7, 29, 56, 67,
　　85, 101, 105, 106
education, 15, 25, 32, 50, 66, 68, 71, 95, 100
egocentrism, 12, 27
electricity, 17-18, 99
energy, 2, 4, 15, 23, 56, 64, 92
endangerment of species, 67, 100
ethics
　　　in business, 78-81
　　　of governments, 75-77
　　　of individuals, 70
　　　of religions, 43, 74-75
evolution, 28, 30, 32, 33, 40, 56, 70, 73, 76, 86, 91, 96, 106
extinction, 12-13, 26, 28, 67
Fadiman, Clifton, 66
Fairfield Pond, 52
false-consensus bias, 28
family planning

  need for, 77-78
  resistance to, 38
Federal Reserve System, 102-103
Festinger, Leon, 56
forest destruction, 2, 5, 11, 12-13, 16, 43, 66, 83, 94
fossil fuels, 4, 12, 21, 29, 64, 65, 66, 67, 83
fracking, 21
French Convention, 47
Gasset, Ortega y, 25, 87
glacier, 4, 14, 29, 84, 85, 92, 99
Global Footprint Network, 16-17, 41-42, 105
global warming 14, 67
Golding, William, 60
Goodall, Jane, 45, 92
Gore, Al, 93
governments
  behavior of, 15, 19, 24, 25, 32, 37, 64, 103
  ethics of, 75-77
  See also "ethics: of governments"
greed, 23, 24, 53, 75-76, 78, 89, 96
greenhouse gases, 2, 4, 29, 81, 85, 98
Grenfell, Julian, 47
Gross domestic product (GDP)
  prioritizing growth, 31, 76, 79, 90, 91, 96, 101-104
  in conflict with environmental protection, 83, 98
  See also "economic growth"
groupthink, 59, 61-64
Guardian, The, 64
Hamlet, 46
Hansen, James, 21
Hiroshima, 20
Hitler, 54
Holdren, John, 7
Howard Hughes Medical Institute, 45, 63
hunters and gatherers, 8, 11, 28, 30, 34, 36, 40, 86
ignorance, 6, 7, 9, 49, 89, 91

imagination, 39-40
Improbable Machine, 54
India, 23, 44, 73-74
indifference to environmental issues, 30
Industrial revolution, 13, 34, 67
inequality of wealth, 21-23, 25, 71
information
    as it influences the thinking process, 7-9, 33, 56, 65, 69, 83, 85
    need for accuracy from the media and government, 37-38, 88-89, 91, 100
    proprietary, 19
    See also "media"
interconnected, 6, 40, 69
    See also "connections": between most human issues
Intergovernmental Panel on Climate Change, 13, 68, 98, 101
IPAT formula, 7-8
irrigation, 11
Islam, see also Muslims, 4, 44, 73
    See also "Muslims"
Jefferson, Thomas, 62
Jonestown massacre, 61-62
journalists, 37, 46, 69, 83, 100
Kristof, Nicholas, 48
Landmesser, August, 62
Lieberman, Daniel, 70
literature
    need for a-fiction to educate about environmental crises, 98-99
    power and influence of, 97
    See also "a-fiction literature"
Madison Avenue, 24, 75, 87, 91, 103
Madison, James, 62
malnutrition, 5, 22, 37
material
    gain, 50

goods, 4, 50, 75
media, 37, 38, 46, 57, 66, 91, 100
methane, 2, 85
migration, 13, 67
mining, 21, 56, 67, 102
money
- as a motivator, 3-4, 32, 38, 46, 49-53, 78, 81, 89
- laundering of, 49
- misuse of, 37

mortality, 34-35
Muslims
- fundamentalist, 55
- genocide of, 44

nanotechnology, 6, 94
National Oceanic and Atmospheric Administration, 14
nature
- damage to, 15, 30, 66-67
- dependence on, 16, 88-90
- disconnect from, 3-5, 86
- feminine, 91, 95
- human, 25, 45, 48

Nazis, 55, 62-63
New York Times, 48
oceans
- acidification of, 13-14, 69
- pollution of, 3, 83
- services provided by, 16

Our Plundered Planet, 66
overload
- of demand, 18
- of issues, 68-70
- of nature, 88

Pacific Lutheran University, 63
peace
- between nations, 20, 24-25
- between religions, 73, 77

        difficulty maintaining, 46-47
        of mind, 44-45, 86
        opposed to violence, 46, 73
        prioritization of, 98, 105
Pearl Harbor, 57
peer pressure, 36, 54-55, 63, 86, 89
perception system
        human, 28-29
        perception of change, 29-31
Perkins, John, 79
Pinker, Steven, 24
politicians
        greed of, 24, 46, 50
        ignorance of challenges, 27, 66, 69, 75
        ignorance of limits to growth, 7, 9, 95-96, 85, 101
        need for, 88, 103-104
        the persuasion of, 38, 91
pollution, 12-13, 21, 65, 67, 83, 101-102
population
        drivers of, 11, 21, 71, 73
        global, 16, 21, 34-35, 37
        impact of, 38, 64, 67, 98
        limits to, 7-8, 12-14, 85, 95, 100-101, 105
        stabilization of, 34, 71-72, 77-78, 101, 104
poverty, 71, 104
power
        as fuel, 2, 18-19, 67
        positions of, 7, 9, 63, 94
        quest for, 32, 46, 49-51, 53, 59-61, 76
        See also "electricity"
primary/primitive human drives and tendencies, 9, 24, 28,
        40-57, 63, 75-76, 88-89
reason
        as a temper for primitive human drives, 9
        lacking in decision-making, 36-39, 64, 88
religion

    as the backbone of ethical behavior, 73-75
    as a driver of terrorism, 43
    treatment of science as, 56
    as a patriarchal system, 94
Rennert, Ira, 52
repetition as a psychological tool, 89
resources
    competition for, 45, 67, 75-76, 92, 106
    cultivation of, 94
    disconnection from 3-4,
    financial, 23, 89
    interconnectedness of, 6
    overconsumption of, 5, 9, 12, 15-17, 41, 67
    reliance on, 15-21
    See also "disconnected" and "interconnected"
revolution
    inevitable, 23
    political, 92
Road to Survival, 66
Robber's Cave Experiment, 60
sawing as method of execution, 48-49
science
    as the way of progress, 54, 89
    environmental, 84
    failure to value, 89
    fiction, 97-98
    ignorance of, 56, 64, 96
    natural, 95, 99
    need to emphasize in education, 95, 97-98
    need to emphasize in journalism, 100
    need to emphasize in politics, 103
scientific method, 87-89
scientists
    developing weapons for tyrants, 63
    distrust of, 52, 64, 83, 96
Scripps Institute of Oceanography, 65

sea-level rise, 13, 26, 29, 68, 76, 83, 84, 95, 98
Selfish Gene, The, 73
selfishness, 50-54, 73, 75
Sherif, Muzafer, 60
short-term
    change, 29-30
    pursuits, 9, 30, 32, 96
    situations, 89
    solutions, 19
    thinking, 98, 105
    winners, 40
slavery, 44, 62
Smith, Adam, 9
Smith, Edward, 84
social psychology, 59-61
Society of Environmental Journalists, 100
sociopaths, 46, 53, 73, 78
special interest groups, 38, 76
Stanford University, 47
steady state economy, 7, 85, 100-106
Storms of my Grandchildren, 21
Storr, Anthony, 45, 55
Story of the Human Body, 70
studying the future, 96-98
survival
    survival instincts, 26, 28, 31, 40, 60, 91
    survival of future generations, 89
sustainability, 15-16, 64, 78, 86, 94, 102
tax, 25, 38-39, 80, 102-103
technology, 3, 6, 8, 15-21, 28, 38, 67, 91
television, 53, 80
Teresa, Vincent, 53
terrorists, 4, 18, 73
tobacco, 80-81
tradition
    as stabilizing social force, 64

        as reinforcing patriarchal structures, 93-95
UC Berkeley, 53
United Nations, 34-36, 71-72
Venus syndrome, 21
violence
        decline of, 24
        human tendency to, 43-49
        in the media, 46
Voght, William, 66
vulnerability to
        electricity and cyber failure, 15, 19
        environmental crises, 21, 67
        nuclear war, 21
        oversimplification, 55
Wackernagel, Mathis, 17
Walton family, the, 22
war
        civil war (Afghanistan), 83
        power tactics, 75-77
        over Golden Calf, 73
        World War I, 47
        World War II, 44, 100
War is a Racket, 78
waste, 3-4, 12, 15, 39, 67
water
        conflicts over, 83
        groundwater, 21
        pollution of, 3, 13, 21, 92
        shortages of, 3, 22, 39, 41, 56, 64, 71, 76-77
        See also "oceans: acidification of"
wealthy
        ecological footprint of, 41-42
        ignorance of big-picture issues, 50-53, 57
        See also "inequality of wealth"
weapons, 19-21, 28, 44, 63, 76
weather events, 13, 30

Wilson, Edward, 28, 30
women
    brutalization of, 45
    empowerment of, 71
    environmentalists, 92-94
    nature of, 48, 95
    right to choose, 38
    roles as leaders, 92-95
World Bank, 102
World Trade Center, 19
Zimbardo, Philip, 47
20/20/20 charity, 52
350.org, 93